HIBAGON

JAPANESE BIGFOOT

2nd Edition

Kyle Brink
K.W. Brink & Daughters, Fukuyama

To my friend A.K.
Scholar, Mentor, Champion of the Poor, &
Hibagon follower from the beginning

ACKNOWLEDGEMENTS

I thank my wife and my daughters for their help.

I thank David Paulides, Harvey Pratt, Melba Ketchum, Steve Isdahl, Scott Carpenter, Wes Germer, Vic Cundiff, MK Davis, ThinkerThunker, Josh Turner, and others working to advance our understanding of bigfoot/hibagon beings.

I thank Mr Paulides for his excellent Missing 411 work. Mr Paulides does not connect his bigfoot work with his missing persons work. I respect this, and have the highest admiration for Mr Paulides. My topics may seem similar, but my focus is local and discrete. My ideas, conclusions, and errors are mine alone.

I thank the Hiroshima Prefectural Police.

I thank the Hiroshima Prefectural Library.

I thank our contributing experts.

I thank Mr Katsuyuki Egi, Ape Clerk.

I thank my Uncle Ray. When this COVID business is over, we are going to go and find that cadaver with ground penetrating radar.

I thank Fuji TV for sharing the cadaver photos.

I thank the families of missing people that have talked and cried with me.

I thank the people of Hiroshima Prefecture for their hospitality to this old varmint hunter. This is one of the greatest places in the whole wide world, maybe only second to Northern Ontario.

1 WELCOME TO THE SECOND EDITION

In the 1st edition I introduced the hibagon to the world, showed the Fuji TV cadaver photos, and shared my thoughts, and the thoughts of experts.

The local media took interest. That was nice. Then the Hiroshima Prefectural Library called. They wanted to preserve my book for posterity. What an honour. But my conscience stung me. You see, I'd been a little too rosey-eyed about the hibagon. Been a bit too much of a flute player and cheerleader. Might have encouraged people to get interested in this magnificent, wonderful, totally peaceful, wise, big forest brother. But I'd learned a lot more since initial publication. Now the thing I want to say above all is this:

BEWARE OF HIBAGON
They take people

Legend told us. Big monsters came down from the mountains and took people to eat them, rape them, or possibly some combination thereof. I believed this went on in the past. But today? It wasn't on the TV news, so it must no longer be happening. The hibagon must have bred and bled their aggression all out, rather like my Japanese friends and neighbours. Who could imagine *their* warlike past? Well, I was right about the Japanese, I hope. Wrong about the hibagon. *They are still taking people, in my opinion.*

The National Police Agency (NPA) of Japan keeps a list of missing persons. These are people who disappeared mysteriously. The police have no ideas. At present there are 336 cases on this list, for a national occurrence rate of 0.264 per 100,000. Twenty-six cases are from Hiroshima Prefecture, or 0.924 per 100,000. So that's 350% the raw national rate. But wait. There are prefectures with high rates, and prefectures with low rates. Let's compare Hiroshima with adjacent Okayama, and with Tokyo.

Hiroshima	(pop. 2,811,410)	26 cases
Okayama	(pop. 1,906,464)	1 case
Tokyo	(pop. 13,960,236)	0 cases

Now consider: [A] Earlier this year, Hiroshima had 24 cases. Now 26. Earlier this year Tokyo had 1 case. Now zero. Look again at those populations.

[B] Hiroshima's crime rate is much lower than Tokyo's. This is not a criminal phenomenon.

[C] Disappearances are in or (more often) adjacent to forests and mountains.

[D] Victims' possessions have been found in inaccessible places. In one case, police pinged a handicapped woman's cell phone. They located it on top of a mountain. With no roads or trails. Then police watched on their screen as the cell phone climbed down and up, and down and up, two more mountains, till it got out of range.

[E] Victims are selected for weakness, i.e. children, the elderly, and the handicapped.

[F] Victims are selected for smallness and lightness, e.g. portability.

[G] Victims leave no blood, suggesting that they are taken with hands, not in teeth.

[H] Victims leave no scent trail, suggesting that they are carried off the ground.

[I] Victims leave no evidence of accident, illness, struggle, or wandering off trail. They simply vanish.

[J] Victims are never found.

[K] Victims disappear under certain sky conditions.

[L] Victims disappear under certain wind conditions.

[M] Victims disappear in regions with strong hibagon (or same thing/different name) legends.

[N] Disappearances occur in clusters.

[O] Disappearances stop at natural borders, e.g. rivers.

[P] Disappearances follow a seasonal pattern.

[Q] Where it is known, victims were taken up mountainsides into remote wilderness, not out by roads toward human habitation.

[R] Victims are not taken when snow is on the ground.

[S] Rain frequently falls during or after disappearances.

[T] Perpetrator has a 100% success rate.

  All of this points to the hibagon. They are not cuddly big ewoks. Nor are they mindless Tasmanian Devils. They are *largely* peaceful, and *most of the time* they want nothing to do with us. But they can be hostile. They have superhuman physical ability, and superhuman intelligence *for their own purposes*. Not to say they write sonnets and piano études, but *in their terrain* they outsmart and outclass you and me in every way. So be smart. Don't go in the woods alone. Don't go unarmed. Be watchful. Keep together, keep together, keep together. Cars kill, but I'm not anti-car. People kill, but I'm not anti-people. I am not anti-hibagon. But hey!
  Let's be careful out there.

Kyle Brink
Fukuyama City, 2021

2 Hello!

The bigfoot research community is a bit like the Star Wars cantina, full of rough and weird and dubious persons, and a few real-solid good guys. Me, I'm just an old varmint hunter from Northern Ontario, blown over to Japan. And what on earth do I have to contribute?

1. The most completely researched and up to date account of the Hibagon: Japanese bigfoot.

2. The Hibagon cadaver[1] photos broadcast 2017 by Fuji TV.

3. A few of my own observations and thoughts on the Hibagon.

4. Solicited expert opinions.

5. Evidence that hibagon are behind many of the mysterious "Missing 411" type disappearances here in Japan.

---

[1] The most appropriate word. A cadaver is a human corpse used for scientific research. Carcass is for animals. Animals cannot interbreed with humans.

How did I get here? Let's review the timeline. *On October 20, 1967*, "Patty" stepped in front of Roger Patterson and Bob Gimlin in Bluff Creek, California. The first bigfoot filmed alive.[2]

Three years later, on July 23, 1970, the Hibagon stepped out of the woods across from the Rokunohara Dam, near Mount Hiba, in Hiroshima Prefecture, Japan. He was seen that day by three municipal employees. The first of dozens of sightings.

Two months after that I sprang into the world! In the thick-with-bigfoot Northern Ontario bush. We already, even back then, had a colossal statue of what we called the sasquatch. It is still there. You can see it from space.

Fast forward. I grew up, hunted varmints, then moved down east, and got a job at a college. Got sent to Hiroshima an exchange program. Fell in

---

[2] There is a photo of a *possible* bigfoot shot dead by trappers in British Columbia, 1894. The back of the photo reads: "YEAR 1894 YALIKOM RIVER AROUND LILLIOTT B.C. FORESTRY - HUDSON BAY CO. THEY TOOK THE PICTURE AND THE GUY THAT WAS IN THE PICTURE WENT & STOLE THEM BACK FROM THE FORESTRY RECORDS (HUDSON BAY CO.) I BELIEVE HIS NAME WAS HOLIDAY (DON'T KNOW THE FIRST NAME) NEVER TOOK ALL THE PICTURES (ONLY ONE) AND TOOK PICTURES OF THE REST. (GLASS PLATE PHOTOGRAPHY)" [The correct spellings are Yalakom River, and Lillooet.] With snowshoes for scale, the dead bigfoot appears to be a juvenile sasquatch. Others see a dead mountain lion. But why would the Hudson Bay Co. steal a picture of a dead mountain lion? And why steal them back?

love with the country and the people. Fell in love with one lady in particular. Fast forward again.

December 28, 2019, I was standing on a wharf in a little fishing village, looking at the sea, when

WHAT THE HELL IS THAT?

I saw a sea serpent. Won't get into it now. I'm just telling you how I got into the Hibagon. Well, I began studying sea serpents, trying to make sense of what I saw. Kept going back to that village as often as I could, to talk with locals and watch the sea. Turned out they had an old legend of a sea serpent god that lived in those waters. They used to worship it. On one of the islands they had a shrine to it. Old local legends, I knew, included the Hibagon. "Well," I thought. "I've already seen the sea serpent. Guess I'd better look into this Hibagon." This is what I found.

- Hibagon and Bigfoot matched up 100%.
- Hibagon was the most *witnessed* bigfoot.
- Hibagon was the most *documented* bigfoot.
- The Hiroshima Police believe he's real.
- Fuji TV broadcast photos of a Hibagon cadaver in 2017.

I got the photos and took them to my best friend, the haematologist. He said the skull was obviously authentic. The bones and vascular structures were correct. Next I showed my dentist buddy. He said the teeth looked real. Very human-like. But too large. I showed the photos to our veterinarian. He took a few days to consult all his books. He came back saying (a) the cadaver was real; (b) it was an unidentified animal. That's when I thought that the North American (and world) bigfoot community should see these photos. They should also have the whole history of the Hibagon, in English.

I felt that I should do this because (a) I live here; (b) I have (just) enough Japanese; (c) bigfoot fascinates me; (d) no one else was doing it; (e) if I didn't do it, who would? So here I am. Instead of "Nice to meet you," I will greet you in the Japanese manner:

よろしくお願ねがいします.

I thank you in advance for your kindness to me.

1894 bigfoot?

Patty

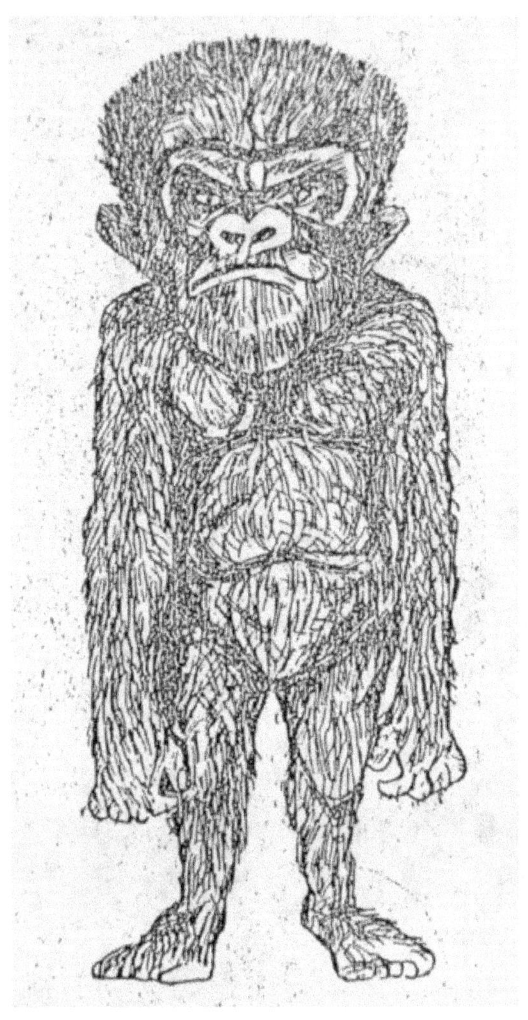

Hibagon, Police forensic sketch

Colossal Bigfoot, Vermillion Bay, Ontario

"High dwellings are the peace and harmony of our descendants. Remember the calamity of the great tsunamis. Do not build any homes below this point."

So say the Tsunami Stones standing around Japan's northeastern coast. Wise words from wise ancestors. Their descendants ignored them. They looked down on the rich, wide floodplains as Lot did on Sodom and Gomorrah, the dollar signs flashing in his eyes. They went down and terraformed that land. They built great cities, with great levees, and floodwalls, and seawalls, and pumping stations. They built beachfront nuclear reactors...

Then along came March 11, 2011, and we saw
what happened. Turns out the ancestors weren't
such ignorant old codgers after all.

Let's apply this. All over Japan, the ancestors
warned of big hairy monsters in the mountains.
They came down at night and took animals and
people for food. They took women for mates.
Sometimes the women came home with hybrid
offspring.

We had similar things in North America. The
Yurok shamaness Che-na-wah Weitch-ah-wha,
a.k.a. Lucy Thompson, called them the Indian
devils: devolved devil monsters that lived in the
mountains. They came to snatch away hapless
Indians, especially the women. Some returned
pregnant. The hybrid offspring would be adopted by
the tribe, but they were never able to assimilate.
They were feral.[3] They always left to join their
fathers. Two cultures, from opposite sides of the
Pacific, describing the same thing.

You know, geologists were studying a megathrust
earthquake in the Cascadia subduction zone, from
northern California up to Vancouver Island. A fault
1000km long slipped 20 meters in an instant (620

____

[3] Lucy Thompson, To the American Indian, 1916. It is
interesting to note that Mrs Thompson's Yuroks were
neighbours of the Hoopa Valley tribe. Cf. David
Paulides, The Hoopa Project: Bigfoot Encounters in
California. Hancock House, 2008. The bigfoot sketched
by forensic artist Harvey Pratt have some very human
faces, supporting Mrs Thompson's account of frequent
interbreeding.

miles, and 66 feet). Dendrochronology, from tree rings in several killed and submerged "ghost forests" dated the earthquake to around the year 1700. Archaeology confirmed this from Indian villages that were buried or abandoned. Indian oral tradition confirmed it. The Huu-ay-ahts said it happened one winter night, shortly after everyone had gone to sleep. The Kwakiutl, the Cowichans, the Macah, and the Quileutes all had stories of houses collapsing and whole villages disappearing. Well, the geologists knew that such a tremendous earthquake would have sent a tsunami clear across the ocean to Japan. The Japanese were literate in 1700. So the geologists went to Japan.

"Yep, we have those records."

A 4-meter (13 foot) tsunami, not locally produced, hit Tōhoku's shores at midnight, January 27, 1700. Tracing the wave back, the geologists dated the Cascadia earthquake to 21:00, December 26, 1700: *a winter night shortly after everyone had gone to sleep.*

These geologists worked with other sciences and other sources, and got things done. If the bigfoot community did this more, we might get more done. High-level multidisciplinary cooperation has occurred once that I know of, in bigfoot studies.[4] Great progress was made. But too many researchers are jealous egotists. They are partly to

---

[4] The great Paulides, Carpenter, Ketchum, et al. DNA studies. A tremendous story. It also confirms Mrs Thompson's account of frequent human-bigfoot interbreeding.

blame for the sad situation in which only 29% of Americans and 21% of Canadians believe that bigfoot is real.

Also at fault are the 71% of Americans and 79% of Canadians who are so self-assured, so smug, that they can call liars (and/or idiots) the thousands of policemen, truckers, farmers, doctors, hunters, soldiers, engineers, judges, housewives, and probably some of my readers. All dismissed, ridiculed, and character-assassinated. My skeptical friends, this is wrong. A man is presumed innocent till proven guilty, I say. Our eyewitnesses are way too consistent and sincere. And this is personal to me, as a sea serpent eyewitness. People on both sides of the Pacific are seeing a being that is:

- Humanoid
- Often described as "apelike"
- Bipedal...
- But also comfortable on all fours
- Covered with hair
- Fingers hang lower than its knees
- Has human-like dentition
- Prognathic
- No neck
- Huge, powerful brow ridge
- Tiny sloped forehead
- Pointed or conical head
- Superhuman musculature and strength
- Superhuman thickness, robustness

Sounds like they're describing the same suspect.

What about his behaviour?

- Generally shy of humans...
- Yet curious…
- With a history of deadly aggression
- Doesn't show fear
- Lives in remote forests and mountains
- Uses cover and camouflage
- Highly intelligent
- Sways side-to-side when agitated
- Uses roads, railroads, transmission tower corridors, rivers etc. for transportation
- Uses stones, tree limbs, etc. as tools/missiles
- Builds stick structures in the woods.
- Eats people
- Reproduces with people.

It doesn't take a PhD in Advanced Bigfootology to conclude that this creature in North America, and this creature in Japan, are the same creature. Logic, economy, common sense, and junior high school biology say so. The Hibagon is the Japanese bigfoot.

Sure, there will be some differences. Take my haematologist and me. We're not identical. He is a *Japanese-type* human, and I am a *European-type* human. He has epicanthic folds in his eyelids; I do not. He has the the mitochondrial rs671 (ALDH2*2) allele resulting in a less functional acetaldehyde dehydrogenase enzyme, responsible for the breakdown of acetaldehyde; I do not, so I can drink him under the table. On the other hand, his 538G>A single-nucleotide polymorphism conked out his ABCC11 gene, meaning he doesn't need to wear antiperspirant; I do. The Japanese spotted Sika deer is the White-tailed deer. The Japanese wild boar is not the American wild boar, yes, yes, yes. You can be a gatherer or a scatterer. Hibagon is the North American bigfoot's Japanese cousin. *And our cousin,* I guess, seeing as how these things can breed with us.

Let's get to know this cousin. But first let's anticipate and deal with some kneejerk objections.

4 OBJECTIONS

OBJECTION 1: Japan is too small for bigfoot.

But it's not. Japan is bigger than Germany, bigger than Finland, bigger than Norway, bigger than Italy, bigger than the UK.

Japan is about as big as California. It is almost as big as Oregon and Washington states combined. It's about as big as British Columbia, west of the Rockies. It is twelve times the size of Vancouver Island. Bigfoot thrive in all these places. Japan is not too small.

OBJECTION 2: Japan is too urban and crowded.

The cities are. But look at the other side of that coin. Forty million Japanese are squashed into greater Tokyo. There's a third of your humans contained, right there. The other two-thirds are mostly crammed into its coastal river plains, leaving a vast wilderness interior = beautiful bigfoot habitat. *Homo sapiens* land use, including farms, is 27% leaving LOTS of room for other species.

The remaining 73% of Japan is uninhabitable and even impenetrable mountains. Japan has 69% forest cover. Only Canada, Russia, Finland, and Sweden come close. The US by comparison is only 47% uninhabited and 36% forested.

OBJECTION 3: People would run into them.

Who? There aren't many hunters in Japan. Hikers? Campers? Loggers? They do predictable things in predictable places. No animal with half a brain is going to "run into" them. The Hibagon has more than half a brain.

Encroachment? The Japanese have already built on every useful scrap of land. The human population is in decline. Rural villages are dying.

You have to think, too, that the geography is different here. It's not like back home. There, when you wanted to go hunting, you just took a walk in the woods. Park your car anywhere, and go on in.

You drive out of the city here, and you are up in the granite mountains. There are no nice gravel shoulders to park your car. *There are no shoulders.* You have at best 1½ lanes with a rock wall on one side, and a sheer drop on the other. Sometimes a guard rail. Where do you want to go? Up? Down?

OBJECTION 4: The Hibagon couldn't hide forever.

Duh, Sherlock. Obviously they don't all stay hidden forever. We have the sightings, and at last we have a body. That's kind of the point of this book. But okay, let's take your average hibagon. Just how well could he hide?

Listen. Even within Tokyo city limits, even to this day, there is unexplored land. Sounds unbelievable, I know. A few years back, a guy discovered a new waterfall. Now think. Waterfalls have no senses. They don't have the gift of locomotion. They aren't cunning. But this thing stayed hidden *in Tokyo* until just a few years ago.

Next door to here, in Onomichi City, there is a famous Buddhist temple called Senkōji. It draws

thousands of tourists and pilgrims every year.
Legend told of a mythical megalith at Senkōji,
called Mirror Rock. But no one had ever seen it. No
one in living memory, anyway. If you went there
and asked the monks, they would have laughed at
you. Silly tourist! There is no Mirror Rock. It is just a
myth.

Oops, they finally found that mythical Mirror Rock,
quite by accident. *It was hidden and lost and
considered a myth for 1,200 years.* Senkōji is
smack downtown. In area, it's only a few city
blocks. Think about this, people. Megaliths can hide
right under our noses downtown, and bigfoot can't
hide in these vast desolate mountains? A little
humility, please. We lose megaliths. Downtown!

We are still finding uncontacted peoples. Whole
tribes, with their own languages and histories and
cultures. Anthropologists say there are hundreds,
maybe thousands of tribes still undiscovered. Why
shouldn't some of these tribes be tribes of bigfoot?[5]

OBJECTION 5: What would they eat?

---

[5] We could speak, too, of Onoda Hiroo, WWII holdout.
Evaded capture in the Philippines for 29 years. The
Japanese government believed there were other
holdouts into the 1990s! Or take Christopher Thomas
Knight. Evaded detection/capture in the woods of Maine
for 27 years. Give Mr Onoda superhuman strength and
superhuman digestion, and see how long he could go in
the jungle then. Give Mr Knight a thick coat of long hair,
and superhuman bulk to conserve body heat, and see
how many more Maine winters *he* could go.

They would eat bamboo (shoots, roots, leaves, stalks); pine trees (nuts, pollen, needles, bark[6]) and other conifers;[7] horsetails, ferns, knotweeds, butterbur, bulbs, mushrooms, berries... My father-in-law had a book on Japan's edible wild herbs. That book was about 800 pages long. Foraging was kind of a hobby for my father-in-law.

The hibagon does it full time. They have sharper senses. They have stronger teeth and jaws and fingernails and everything. They have stronger stomachs. They can go anywhere. How thick do you think *their* book of edible herbs is?

For protein they have insects, grubs, frogs, snakes, birds, birds' eggs, fish, shellfish, pets, and livestock. And human trash. But above all, the very plentiful, very delicious deer and wild boar.

Mrs Lucy Thompson tells how her people, a tribe of several thousands, lived very well from foraging and hunting in a semi-arid, Mediterranean climate. Hiroshima is humid and subtropical. More flora, supporting more fauna. As a grizzled old varmint hunter, let me tell you. If Japan let me have guns, I could feed my family on wild boar and never need to buy meat again.

I live in the centre of a city of half a million people. *Near my house* there are warning signs.

---

[6] Bark is commonly eaten by primates for its high sugar and protein content. Austrolopithacus ate bark, we know from coprolites.

[7] Brendza, "Eating Pine - How to Eat a Pine Tree to Survive."

In the suburbs, I have friends who don't go out after dark because of hogs. Up in the mountains, hogs are ripping up the fields. My mother-in-law can't get rid of them.

One more thing. We have black bears here. Just last month, a man got bit on his face by one. If bears can support themselves here, Hibagon can.

OBJECTION 6: A breeding population would require too much space.

Mountain gorillas have an average troop home range of 8 square miles.[8] Neanderthal man had an estimated home range (for an active network of 145 individuals) of 20 square miles.[9]

Hiroshima Prefecture is 8,479 square kilometers = 3,273 square miles. Seventy-three percent is uninhabited.[10] So that's 2,389 uninhabited square

---

[8] National Geographic.com

[9] Dunbar, Gamble, and Gowlett, Lucy to Language: The Benchmark Papers, Oxford University Press.

[10] Hiroshima is exactly the national average. That's a little over 2,000,000 acres of uninhabited mountains, here in Hiroshima Prefecture. For Canadian readers, that is a little bigger than Algonquin Provincial Park, which is known bigfoot habitat. For US readers, that is almost 3 times bigger than Yosemite National Park, also known bigfoot habitat. Reference the video of four bigfoot stalking bison, taken by an official Yosemite National Park webcam. For a great analysis and breakdown, I recommend the YouTube video "Bigfoot vs

miles: enough space for 119 active networks of Neanderthals (17,255 individuals) or 298 mountain gorilla troops (2,682 individuals).

It is assumed that these Neanderthals and gorillas lived entirely off the land. They had no cornfields, rice paddies, apple orchards, and vegetable gardens to steal from. No garbage dumps or rubbish bins. No chicken coops to raid. All of these human resources (plus humans ourselves, I'm afraid) would allow for larger numbers. So there's lots of space for several dozen or several hundred hibagon. Hey, if you don't believe me, you go hiking up in these mountains for a week. Tell me then that there's not enough land. And we're still only talking about Hiroshima. Japan has 46 more prefectures.

OBJECTION 7: Why haven't they been seen since 1982?

I think they are still being seen. Just not being reported. We know that most bigfoot sightings go unreported. Yeah, that's too bad. Because bullying objectors like you have them all running scared. Yes. Most people don't enjoy getting laughed at and called idiots and liars. They don't enjoy losing friends and relatives, sometimes their spouses. People are afraid to lose their jobs. That's in North America, home of so-called freedom of speech.

Here in Japan, freedom of speech isn't even much of a thing. "The nail that sticks up gets hammered down." If in America a minority of sightings gets

---

Buffalo (ThinkerThunker)," by ThinkerThunker.

reported, here it will be a minority of a minority of a minority.

Imagine this. You grow up in Japan. Let's just say you're a Japanese girl. Your hair has a tint of natural brown. Your school can make you dye it black or be expelled.[11] Your hairstyle, too, had better be one of the approved styles, or you might get your head shaved.[12] Your student handbook has a list of activities (chewing gum, wearing make-up, riding a skateboard, etc.) that are forbidden everywhere and at all times, even at home and on weekends. Your handbook tells you what underwear you can wear. "Being mindful of hygiene, always wear white underwear. Do not wear underwear with colours or prints."[13] Now line up over there, tallest to shortest, for your daily bra strap inspection.[14] And don't complain. This is the easiest time of your life.[15] Now then. Does this

---

[11] Japan Today, "Tokyo public schools will stop forcing students to dye their hair black, official promises." August 4, 2019.

[12] Japan Times, "Students and teachers have mixed views on Japanese schools' strict dress and hair codes." May 30, 2019.

[13] Sora News 24, "Tokyo junior high school demands students wear white underwear as part of dress code." October 27, 2016.

[14] Sore News 24, "Japanese middle school criticized for pulling out girls' bra straps to check their color." November 17, 2020.

[15] Mothership, "Japanese worker fired for being out of frame during Zoom video call." May 22, 2020. The university graduate was one month into his first job. Fear of the COVID-19 coronavirus had prompted the

environment encourage people to report monster sightings? I can tell you firsthand, it does not.

But let me ask you this. Why didn't we see the Hibagon cadaver photos until now? The locals had them for decades. They weren't exactly keeping them Top Secret. But they weren't exactly advertising them, either. The folks up here in the mountains of Hiroshima—they're pretty much like the folks up in Northern Ontario, or the folks up in West Virginia. They're friendly and generous, but they don't want trouble, and they might be a little slow to open up to strangers, and basically, they mind their own beeswax. No one saw the photos because no one asked. But the photos were there. I'm pretty sure that's how it is with sightings. Don't ask, don't tell.

OBJECTION 8: But Japan has a long history. Why did no one record these creatures before 1970?

This is actually the most interesting objection to me. "Bigfoot" was never recorded until September

---

company to train its recruits online. They terminated this rogue right quick for "bad manners during online training." It seems that sometimes his chin was out of frame. Exacerbating matters, the impertinent scoundrel was wearing a cardigan over his dress shirt. From Teller Report, "After 24 years of his appointment, an employee in Japan was fired for concealing that he had a university degree." August 23, 2020. He was by all accounts a fine employee. After 24 years of good service, you'd think they'd forgive the poor guy for being overqualified. Not in Japan.

21, 1958. That's when Andrew Genzoli of the
Humboldt Times gave the name (actually "Big
Foot") to the creature. That's surprisingly recent,
isn't it? "Big Foot" predates "Hibagon" by only 12
years.[16] But of course bigfoot were seen and
recorded prior to 1958. By J.W. Burns in 1929; by
Theodore Roosevelt in 1889 in *The Wilderness
Hunter.* You had the Mississipi Wild Man of 1868;[17]

---

[16] *Sasquatch* enters English (from Salish) in 1929, in
J.W. Burn's article "Introducing B.C.'s Hairy Giants,"
Maclean's: "The strange people, of whom there are but
few now—rarely seen and seldom met—are known by
the name of Sasquatch, or, 'the hairy mountain men.'"
[17] Hunters followed their dogs on the trail of an unknown
animal till they came to footprints in the mud. The prints
"appeared similar to the track of a human foot, and they
observed also that the toes of one foot turned
backward." When the hunters caught up to their baying
pack, they "beheld a frightful looking creature, of about
the average height of man, but of far greater muscular
development, standing menacingly in front o f the dogs.
It had long hair flowing from its head, reaching to it [sic]
knees; its entire body, also, seemed to be covered with
hair of two to three inches in length, which was of a dark
brown color. From its upper jaw projected two very large
tusks, several inches long." When the dogs attacked, "it
reached forward and grabbed one of them,...pressed its
tusks, pierced it through and killed it instantly." The
hunters fired several shots. The creature jumped into the
Mississippi River and stayed submerged for several
minutes. Then it surfaced, "uttering shrieks which almost
petrified the pursuers with terror. No similar sound had
ever come to the ears of the men, who were all familiar
with the howl of the wolf, the whine of the panther, and
the hoarse bellowing of the alligator. After sinking and
rising several times, it swam to the Louisiana shore and
disappeared." It was later reported near Vicksburg and

the Ohio Wild Man of 1856;[18] the Vermont Wild Man of 1851[19] (known since at least 1831); the Arkansas Wild Man of 1846, and so on. Many such cases. Not to mention the Wild Girl of Catahoula.[20]

Meadeville. The Cambria Freeman.

[18] Believed to have been a feral man, perhaps a survivor of the 1811-1812 New Madrid Earthquake. A search party was organized. The first man to find him chased him out across the frozen Brant Lake, and tried to capture him. Bad idea. "The wild man...bounded upon him, dragged him from the saddle, and tore him in a dreadful manner, gouging one of his eyes, and biting a large piece out of his shoulder. He then threw the saddle and bridle from the horse and mounted. He set off for the mountains at full speed, guiding the horse with a piece of sapling." The wild man was described as "an athletic man about six feet four inches high, covered with hair of a brownish cast." Ashland Union.

[19] Two men saw something "bearing the unmistakable likeness of humanity" chasing a herd of cattle. "He was of gigantic stature, the body being covered with hair, and the head with long locks that fairly enveloped his neck and shoulders." The creature, found out, stopped and stared at the men before running into the woods "with great speed, leaping from twelve to fourteen feet at a time." Vermont Watchman and State Journal.

[20] "They say she is one of the most ferocious-looking beings that the human eye was ever cast upon...She is as fleet as a deer, and at one leap she cleared a root seven feet high. She uses no language, only gibberish." St. Paul Daily Globe, August, 1888. Witnesses Capt. J.M. Ball and J.C. Goulden, two men of good repute, described her as "a white female without clothes and would seem to weigh about 140 pounds and as active as a cat...covered with hair varying in length in different parts of her." St. Martinville Weekly Messenger, November, 1888. On this occasion the girl was carrying a pig in one hand, and an "old knife" in her other hand.

The same thing in Japan. Hibagon have been here all along. Seen and talked about all along. They have just been called by different names. But they're described the same way: big, monkey-like monsters coming out of the forest, and stealing and eating people and raping women and making babies with them.

The Wild Girl was last reported in upper Franklin Parish in 1891. She was described as being very powerful, covered with hair, and carrying a knife or sword.

5 HIBAGON MYTHOLOGIZED

Anthropologist and primatologist David Daegling says it is strong evidence for bigfoot that the "legend" existed before there was a single name for the creature.[21] Regular people get this. In a bigfoot presentation that I made for Japanese, people were more impressed by the anthropological evidence—the American Indians' bigfoot names, bigfoot masks, bigfoot totem poles—than they were by the photos and films. Scattered across a continent, divided by geography, language, and culture, the Indian tribes *independently* came up with their own names for bigfoot, and their own pictures of him. Like the Hairy Man pictograph at Painted Rock, the Tule River Indian Reservation (near Hoopa). Reminds me of the dinosaur pictographs and petroglyphs from as far flung points as Cambodia and Northern Ontario, but that is *quite* another story. Here are a few of the Indian names for bigfoot, translated:

- Chinook: The Evil God of the Woods
- Shoshone: Cannibal Giant
- Zuni: Cannibal Demon
- Kwakwaka'wakw: Wild Man of the Woods
- Quinault: Devil of the Forest
- Cherokee: Hairy Savage
- Choctaw: Monster Giant
- Kashehotapalo: Cannibal Man

---

[21] David Daegling, "Bigfoot Exposed: An Anthropologist Examines America's Enduring Legend," p.28.

- Chickasaw: Smelly, Hairy Being that can Speak
- Athabascan: Wicked Cannibal
- Tsonaquaw: Wild Woman of the Woods
- Coast Salish: Wild Man of the Woods

Even in English, we still can't agree on one name. "Bigfoot" beats "sasquatch" three to one.[22] It beats "skunk ape" seventy to one. But these alternative names persist, along with boogers, booger men, boogie men, brushmen, hill monkeys, holla yellas, grassmen, swamp cabbage men, stink apes, skunk demons, skoocooms, timber giants, wild men, wood men, and many others. Sometimes the names are fixed to a particular location: The Devil's Creek Monster, The Fouke Monster, The Cole Hollow Monster, The Mogollon Monster, The Bennington Monster (a.k.a. The Glastenbury Monster), the Portlock Monster, the Traverspine Gorilla, The Blood Beast of Monster Mountain, and so on. A lot of different names, but they all refer to the same basic creature. Strong evidence because multiple and independent. Could similar evidence from multiple independent sources be found in Japan?

Yes. I looked through Japanese legends and myths and ancient texts, and I found the Hibagon hiding under several different names:

---

[22] Which is why I use bigfoot in this book, although I prefer sasquatch.

- *ENKO.* From right here in Hiroshima Prefecture. Hairy monsters, resembling large monkeys. Used rivers to crawl in and out of human villages. Once abducted a human woman who later returned and gave birth to a monstrous monkey-like baby. The villagers burned it. In Geishu City, these creatures were called KAWASARU, lit. "river monkeys." Said to have the strength of 100 men.

- *KAKUSARU, lit. "*black monkeys." Monkey-like bipedal creatures 1.6 meters in height. They live in the mountains. Like the enko, they kidnap human women and reproduce with them. Women whom they fail to impregnate, they release. The others they keep. From the encyclopedic *Wakan Sansai Zue* (1712): *"A kakusaru is like a big black monkey, with long hair, and standing and walking. He understands the human language and reads the human mind, so even if a person tries to kill the kakusaru, the kakusaru escapes quickly and can never be caught."* At a place near the Izumi River, Gifu Prefecture (currently Motoso City), a woman fought off a kakusaru with her sickle. Villagers followed the blood trail into the mountains, and then lost it in the dark of night.

- *KUROTE.* "Black Hand." The proper name given to an individual monster in the 16th century. In Ishikawa Prefecture, the wife of

Kasamatsu Jingobei was going to the toilet, which at that time was a trapdoor in the raised floor. From underneath the house, a huge hand reached up and groped her. She screamed, understandably. Jingobei grabbed his sword, ran in, and cut off the monster's hand. The monster was described as monkey-like, hairy all over, and nine shaku in height (nearly nine feet).

Pause the lesson while you go and use our Edo-era toilet. Step 1: Put on these toilet slippers. Step 2: Remove the trapdoor. Step 3: Pull up your kimono. Step 4: Straddle the hole. Step 5: Hang onto handlebars for dear life. Beneath you is the river. Beneath poorer folks is a ditch, a cart, a basket, or a pig enclosure. Step 6: Do your business. Step 7: Wipe with the family wiping stick (not pictured). Step 8: Replace trapdoor. Okay?

And you're back. Oops, you're still wearing the toilet slippers. Those stay in the toilet. They're for everyone to use, okay? No need to feel embarrassed. All right, so let's continue with our lesson.

- *SATORI.* Apelike monsters in the mountains of Gifu Prefecture. They are said to read men's minds.[23] They have been known to kill and eat humans, but more often they avoid contact.
- *IKEMONO.* "Foreign hairy beast." They are larger than humans, covered in long hair, and look like monkeys. Live high up in the mountains of Niigata Prefecture, but come down to the valleys to find food.

These all sound like bigfoot. Note the aggression, the rape of women, and the production of hybrid offspring.

Now let's see how these prefectures do on the National Police Agency's list of mysteriously missing persons. Again, as a baseline, Tokyo's rate is .000. Prefectures adjacent to Tokyo are Saitama at .081, Yamanashi at .122, Kanagawa at .187, and Chiba at .063. These are largely urban prefectures with high crime rates and no hibagon traditions.

The rate for Hiroshima (ENKO, KAWASARU, HIBAGON) is again .924. Conjoined prefectures

---

[23] I don't know what to do with the stories of bigfoot telepathy or "mindspeak," but this reminds me of that.

are Yamaguchi at .871, Tottori at .525, Shimane at .601, and Okayama, well separated by the Ashida and Nariwa Rivers, at .052.[24]

The rates for Ehime and Kagawa (on the island of Shikoku, facing Hiroshima) are .894 and .526. Facing the other way, to the Pacific, are Tokushima and Kochi, .137 and .000.

In central Japan, the rate for Gifu (KAKUSARU, SATORI) is .753. The rate for adjacent Toyama (connected by forest and mountain) is .670. The rate for Ishikawa (KUROTE) is .701. Ishikawa borders Toyama, making a vast hibagon corridor.

In the north, the rate for Niigata (IKEMONO) is .763. Adjacent Gunma is .774. Tochigii has an ominous .411.

The prefecture with the highest rate of cases on the National Police Agency's list of mysteriously missing persons is Nara, at 1.361. Nara is also the prefecture with the lowest amount of habitable land (10% habitable by humans). It also is rich with traditions of bipedal cannibal monsters in its mountains, called oni. We will get to them in a minute.

More suspects from Japanese folklore:

- *Ammo.* Hairy, live in the mountains of Iwate Prefecture, and emit a bad odor.

---

[24] The phenomenon appears to stop at a natural barrier, the Ashida River, in eastern Hiroshima. Okayama's one case occurred in the north of the prefecture, above the headwaters of this river.

- *Daidarabotchi.* Gigantic monsters who leave gigantic footprints in the mountains.
- *Hachishaku-sama.* An 8-foot tall woman that kidnaps stray human children.
- *Hihi.* A baboon-like creature in the mountains.
- *Jami.* Wicked mountain spirits.
- *Kawaakago.* A half-human creature that pretends to be a crying baby in order to lure its victims into the forest.
- *Onikuma.* Literally, Devil bear. Upright walking, bear-like creatures who sneak down from the mountains into villages at night, and carry off livestock for food. They also throw stones, greater than ten people together could move.
- *Keukegen.* The character for "hair" appears twice in the name of this being, emphasizing its hairiness. Even the females are covered with hair. They live in the mountains and eat pine needles.
- *Otoroshi.* Bipedal beasts covered with long hair, and with manes of messy hair. They are masters of concealment, and are seen only when they want to be seen. They eat horses and cattle. They live in caves. Their name means scary, frightening, or dishevelled.
- *Yōkai shidaidaka.* Giant mountain-dwelling humanoids who steal hunters' kills.
- *Uba.* Man-sized, hairy, bipedal monsters. Legend says they used to be human.

- *Waira.* Mountain-dwelling giants.
- *Yamauba.* "Mountain ogres." Covered in hair, live in the mountains, and eat human flesh. They sometimes steal children.
- *Yokubo.* Mountain-dwelling giants who mimic and shout back to human travelers.
- *Ouni*[25]—also called the *wauwau*[26]—a mountain yōkai with the face of a *hag*, with a mouth that reaches from ear to ear, and a body entirely covered in hair. They appear at mountain streams. They are highly territorial and dangerous to humans. They move with incredible speed. They have, I say, the gape-mouthed face of a *hag*, please remember, and they are covered all over in hair.

The tendency of the Japanese to mythologize and idolize should never be underestimated. I have a friend who worships a Billiken doll.[27] Since 1970, the Japanese have mythologized and deified the Hibagon. Friends have said to me the following:

- "Hibagon? Oh, yes. Isn't that a *yōkai?*" [A *yōkai* is a mythical spirit or minor deity.]

------

[25] In the monster scrolls of Toriyama Sekien (1712-1788).
[26] Sawaki Suushi, in his 1737 Hyakkai Zukan, or "Illustrated Volume of a Hundred Demons," a bestiary of Japanese monsters.
[27] A doll made by the Billiken Company of Chicago. Was a big fad in the early 1900s.

- "Hibagon? I heard he is the guardian *yōkai* of the mountain."
- "Yes, I know Hibagon. He is the god of Mount Hiba."

These are educated, 21st-century people. They are describing the hibagon as a god. Fifty years ago, the newspapers made no such claim. Hibagon was always described as a flesh and blood animal. My point is this. If my friends and neighbours can *deify* the Hibagon in the space of fifty years, what on earth were their illiterate bumpkin ancestors doing for hundreds of years? Would it surprise us to find hibagon (under another name) *deified* in temples and shrines up and down the length of this land? I propose that this should not surprise us. We probably ought to predict it. Now here is my #1 top candidate for hibagon/bigfoot by another name:

6 THE ONI

Oni (usually translated as devil, as in "Indian devil") are all over Japan. The word 隠 is from the root "to hide or conceal." Reminds me of the Yakima Indian name for bigfoot: *Spirit Hidden by Woods*. Besides hiding in the woods, what else does the oni share with bigfoot?

- Gigantic humanoid creature or wild man
- Fearsome
- Covered in long wild hair
- Has hands, not paws
- Lives in wilderness, mountains
- Superhuman strength and stamina
- Intelligent and cunning
- Mimics animals, humans
- Smells bad
- Mischievous or outright evil
- Abducts people
- Eats people
- Carries a wooden club. Compare with bigfoot tree knocking.

What, if anything, does the oni *not* share with bigfoot?

- Later representations have horns and fangs.
- Later representations come in vibrant colours: red, blue..

- Later representations carry a spiked *kanabō* iron war club used by samurai in feudal Japan.
- Later representations wear a loincloth.

Notice that the first list is longer than the second. Also, the second list is true of *later* representations. They are fantastical accretions, embellishments.

Recall that the prefecture with the highest rate of mysteriously missing persons is Nara (1.361). David Paulides has taught us to be mindful of geographic place names "Devil's Creek," "Devil's Peak," and so on. Look at a map of Nara. It is rich with names like "Oni Mountain," "Oni's Cutting Board," and "Oni's Toilet." Visit Nara's historic temples and shrines. They are full of oni statues.

Take this antique oni ritual exorcism mask (pictured in a few moments) with its wide gaping mouth. Huge, human-like teeth. Massive bottom jaw with enormous ramus. Wide, flared nose. Large round eyes. Enormous brow ridge. Low, sloped forehead. Hint of a conical head or sagittal crest. Hairy. It is ticking off my hibagon checklist.

Now take this Sts'ailes Indian sasquatch mask. Huge, wide gaping mouth. Massive bottom jaw with enormous ramus. (Teeth not shown.) Wide, flared nose. Large round "googly" eyes.[28] Strong brow ridge. Low, sloped forehead. Top of head covered with hair. Hairy all over. Ticking the same boxes.

---

[28] "Googly" eyes or bug eyes were sometimes reported of Hibagon.

Enko, Kawasaru, Satori, etc. are regional names for the hibagon. Oni is the standard common word. Here are two examples from Japan's northern and southern tips. First from the Akakurayama Shinto Shrine in Aomori, way up north:

Worshippers believe that Mount Akakura is inhabited by a multitude of oni, who pose particular dangers to those undertaking shugyo (ascetic discipline) on its slopes. Oni may call out the name of unwary ascetics climbing the mountain, and possess them. Various sites on the mountain have strong associations with oni, including the "Lookout of the Oni," and the "Oni Sumo Ring." The nearby "Oni Jinja" (Oni Shrine) is dedicated to these complex beings, especially the figure of Onigamisama, considered by many to be the original presiding spirit of the mountain. As elsewhere in Japan, oni were formerly venerated as indigenous divinities and are now widely regarded as subjugated, dangerous figures. This oni mask is stored on the altar of the Shinden (inner sanctuary).

The next passage comes from Kunisaki Buddhists in Kyushu, the southernmost main island. Note, these are totally different religions, at opposite geographical extremes.

...In Kunisaki, oni and people are connected like life-long friends...The mysterious mass of misty mountains is covered in fog with a strange miasma, and one can't help but feel this eerie place houses oni. The truth is, oni really did reside here. Cliff ridges spread across the round peninsula in a radial pattern

and you can find caves in these rock formations. Furthermore, these caves are located in positions which are inaccessible to humans. Only unimaginably strong oni could have lived in those locations. Once upon a time, Kunisaki was a magical land part of another world, where oni roamed. Like the legend of the oni who breaks large rocks with brute force, and makes them into stone steps in one night, Kunisaki is full of oni tales...The oni of Kunisaki use their mystical power to prevent hardship and disaster, and are thus fervently worshipped by the people…

Monks play a key role in the deep and strong friendship between people and oni. Monks have always looked up to the oni in a way, because of the mystical power the oni has possessed since the days of old. Ancient Buddhist monks established "mineiri," a training that involves making their way around grottos built into the cliff ridges. The grottos were originally built when the monks went searching for the oni high in the ridges long ago. The halls and shrines may not be there, but the idea of naturally coming in contact with the deities in these mystical caves has been part of Kunisaki's history for 1000 years. Many of the grottos are called "okunoin," and they are considered the origins of faith by every temple. Before long, in the six localities of Kunisaki, up to 65 temples were built, and the Buddhist culture of "Rokugo Manzan" was established. Most of these temples created masks of oni, where priests would dress up as oni. These rituals prayed for everything from national peace and security to rainmaking. And just like that, the culture of praying to oni took root in Kunisaki. Presently, even at temples that no longer

It's like this all over Japan. This cultural evidence
may not prove anything to the hardened tough-guy
too cool for school skeptic. But to *you*, my sensible
and sensitive reader, it *does* establish that the
Japanese have multiple, independent, ancient
accounts of large, hairy, bipedal, bigfoot-looking,
bigfoot-behaving, man-eating, woman-raping
creatures in the mountains. They name places after
them. They have festivals to celebrate or appease
them. They *worship* them. I want you to see that
Hibagon did not appear in a vacuum.

Again, like that transoceanic tsunami, the oni or
hibagon or bigfoot, whatever you call him, is
experienced by widely separated peoples. Take
that poor Hiroshima woman abducted and
impregnated by an enko. Put her aside Seraphine
Long from Harrison Lake, British Columbia. These
women never communicated. Never conspired to
tell tall tales.

*I was walking toward home one day many years ago
carrying a big bundle of cedar roots and thinking of
the young brave Qualac (Thunderbolt) that I was soon
to marry. Suddenly, at a place where the bush grew*

close and thick beside the trail, a long arm shot out and a big hairy hand was pressed over my mouth. Then I was suddenly lifted up into the arms of a young sasquatch. I was terrified, fought, and struggled with All my might. In those days, I was strong. But it was no good, the wild man was as powerful as a young bear. Holding me easily under one arm, with his other hand he smeared tree gum over my eyes, sticking them shut so that I could not see where he was taking me.

He then lifted me to his shoulder and started to run. He ran on and on for a long long time, up and down hills, through thick brush, across many streams never stopping to rest.Once he had to swim a river and then perhaps I could have gotten away, but I was so afraid of being drowned that I held on tightly with my arms about his neck. Although I was frightened I could not but admire his easy breathing, his great strength and speed of foot. After reaching the other side of the river, he began to climb and climb. Presently the air became very cold. I could not see but I guessed that we were close to the top of a mountain. At last the sasquatch stopped hurrying, then he stooped over and moved slowly as if feeling his way along a tunnel.

Presently he laid me down very gently and I heard people talking in a strange tongue I could not understand. The young giant next wiped the sticky tree gum from my eyelids and I was able to look around me...A small fire in the middle of the floor gave all the light there was. As my eyes became accustomed to the gloom I. saw that beside the young giant who had brought me to the cave there were two other wild people, a man and a woman.

To me, a young girl, they seemed very very old, but they were active and friendly and later I learned that they were the parents of the young sasquatch who had stolen me. When they all came over to look at me

I cried and asked to go home. They just smiled and shook their heads. From then on I was kept a close prisoner; not once would they let me go out of the cave. Always one of them stayed with me when the other two were away. They fed me well on roots, fish and meat. After I had learned a few words of their tongue, which is not unlike the Douglas dialect, I asked the young giant how he caught and killed the deer, mountain goats and sheep that he often brought into the cave. He smiled, opening and closing his big hairy hands. I guessed that he just laid in wait and when an animal got close enough, he leapt. He was certainly big enough, quick enough and strong enough to do so.

When I had been in the cave for about a year I began to feel very sick and weak and could not eat much. I told this to the young sasquatch and pleaded with him to take me back to my own people. At first he got very angry, as did his father and mother but I kept on pleading with them, telling them that I wished to see my own people again before I died. I really was ill and I suppose they could see that for themselves because one day after I cried for a long time, the young sasquatch went outside and returned with a leaf full of tree gum. With this he stuck down my eyelids as he had done before. Then he again lifted me to his big shoulder.

The return journey was like a very bad dream for I was light headed and in much pain. When we re-crossed the wide river, I was almost swept away; I was too weak to cling to the young sasquatch but he held me with one big hand and swam with the other. Close to my home, he put me down and gently removed the tree gum from my eyelids. When he saw that I could see again he shook his head sadly, pointed to my house and then turned. My people were all wildly excited when I stumbled back into the house for they had long ago given me up as dead. But I was too sick and weak to talk. I just managed to crawl into bed and that night I gave birth to a child. The little one lived only a few hours, for which I have always been thankful. I hope that never again shall I see a sasquatch.

Put the two women together with the Maid and the Wild Man of Yallam. From 18th century Dorset, England:

She stole away when the night was still,
Wearing her prettiest clothes,
Up to the beeches on Yellowham Hill
To meet with a wild wose.
Fierce he was, and covered in hair,
With a gleam in his ancient eye.
He beckoned her into his leafy lair
With a smile that made her sigh.
At morn she rose with blushing cheeks,
And fled home to her father's mill.
She tarried there some forty weeks,
Then went back to the woods on Yellowham Hill.
Up she climbed with a green-haired child,
And down she came alone from the wose's wild.

Indulge me a little more. Yes, we are in Europe now. The Wild Man is on the coat of arms of Antwerp; the royal coat of arms of Denmark, and the former Kingdom of Greece. The coat of the arms of Prussia, and the arms of towns all through Germany: Naila, Neuhof an der Zenn, Schwarzburg-Rudolstadt, and the aptly named Wildemann in the Upper Harz, founded 1529 by miners who met a wild man and his wild wife in the wild Harz mountains. The Wild Man is on the coat arms of Lapland, and several cities in Finland. He is on the personal coat of arms of Prince Philip, Duke of Edinburgh. The Wild Man is in literature, painting, folklore, architecture, engravings...you find him embroidered in the Great Wardrobe of Edward III. And what does he look like?

- Scary, gigantic wild man
- Covered with long hair
- Lives in wild mountains
- Enormous strength and stamina
- Intelligent
- Mischievous-to-evil
- Abducts people
- Eats people.
- Has a wooden club

  Take the Rochester Cathedral Green Man: Huge, wide gaping mouth. Massive bottom jaw with enormous ramus. Human-like teeth. Wide, flared nose. Large round eyes. Enormous brow ridge. Low, sloped forehead. Top of head covered with hair. Hairy. He is checking our checklist.

  We see these things through different cultural distorting goggles, and we give them different names. Go to the other end of the Eurasian continent. Across the East China Sea from here,

your regular Chinese peasant calls them, 野人,
"wild man," but his Communist Chinese overlords
refer to them officially as 直立高等灵长目奇异动物:
"upright higher primate strange animal." Same
thing, different story.

Here are some pictures. Please keep in mind that
these painters and wood carvers are going off of
3rd-hand descriptions. They have to use their own
imaginations. This gives us wildly differing visual
representations. So please make allowances for
that. Ever seen a medieval painting of an elephant
or a giraffe? Heck, have you ever seen a medieval
painting of an oyster?

Satori

A friendly uba

Ouni: Gazu Hyakki Yagyo, Toriyama Sekien

Wauwau: Hyakki Zukan, Sawaki Suushi

Hibagon? See fleeing man for scale

Ritual oni exorcism mask, Freer Gallery of Art

Sts'ailes Indian sasquatch mask

Prince Philip's coat of arms

Dietrich von Bern fighting a Wild Man

Albrech Dürer: Wild Men

Green Man, Rochester Cathedral

Schongauer Wild Man

Schongauer Wild Woman

A medieval oyster

7 MOUNT HIBA

The Chūgoku Mountain range is the backbone of western Japan. These granite mountains run east-west for 500 kilometers, forming a watershed and natural barrier between the *Sannin* region on the Sea of Japan, and the *Sanyō* region on the Seto Inland Sea. From a distance, they look like the La Cloche and Nor'Wester Mountains of Northern Ontario.

Get up into them, however, and they have that crazy steepness that you see in Chinese and Japanese scroll paintings. Verticalness, and steepness, and remoteness that you can't compare with anything in the Western hemisphere. Slices of sky, and canyons of rock. Vertical cliffs and bottomless gorges. And it is just as well that you cannot enter these gorges because they are full of gigantic spiders, venomous snakes,[29] and double-jawed land leeches hanging from trees.

Mount Hiba (Hibayama, 比婆山) is the 10th highest mountain in this range. It is in the city limits of Shobara (population 33,650) in northern Hiroshima prefecture. Total area of this rural

---

[29] Father-in-law used to make a pit viper liqueur. Take a pit viper, and put him alive in a plastic jug of 40% clear alcohol. Hang the jug in a sunny place and watch for several days, until very sure the pit viper is dead. Wait a few more days to be sure, then drink. Thank me later.

municipality is 1,246 km². Enough habitat for 60 troops of wild gorillas (720 individuals), or 24 colonies of independent Neanderthals (3,480 individuals). Actually more, with diets supplemented with stolen rice and corn, stolen livestock, and of course stolen people.

The main industry here is mining (rouseki clay, pyrophyllite, kaolinite, talc, limestone.)[30] Hiba and nearby mountains are also rich with iron sand. This is the birthplace of Japanese ironware.[31]

The second industry is agriculture. Fruit, vegetables, and rice.[32] Grassy tablelands support cattle for wagyu beef. Streams and rivers support extensive rice farming and saké-making. All of this helps to support the native hibagon.

Shobara is one of the coldest places in western Japan. It gets snowfalls exceeding 100 cm and winter totals of over five meters.[33]

---

[30] Shokozan Mining Co., Ltd. is the largest limestone miner in all of Japan.

[31] All those mining tunnels...pretty attractive if you are a mountainous cave dweller.

[32] All those orchards and gardens and rice paddies...pretty attractive if you are large and calorie hungry.

[33] That difficult access...pretty attractive if you shun human company. If you were all covered in thick hair, and you found the right cave or discarded mine tunnel, you could enjoy wine-cellar temperatures year round. Feed on wild boar, making the odd nocturnal raid on

Okay. Now let's talk about the vortex of weirdness that is Mount Hiba.

THE MEGALITHS

The mountain is littered with megaliths older than Japan and the Japanese people. The stones were here before the Jomon and Yamato people arrived. Archaeologists cannot read the occasional carved scripts. The Japanese believe these megaliths to mark "power spots," in a system reminiscent of ley lines. Shintoists and Buddhists both build shrines and temples around them. So megaliths in themselves are quite common. But it is rare to see so many in one location. And several of these are unique in shape and (presumed) function.

One is called the "Chōzubachi Rock." A *chōzubachi* is a bowl or basin at the entrance of a Shinto shrine, used for ceremonial washing of one's hands. This is a great bathtub-sized, carved out stone. Very probably part of some ancient purification ritual.

Nearby is a structure of boulders thought to be an "offering stand" or altar.

There is a group of rectangular pillars, some still standing, and many knocked or fallen down. Rumoured to mark the buried treasure of Emperor Jimmu, first legendary emperor of Japan.[34] This grouping is called the "Holy War Rocks."

---

nearby orchards. Sounds like quite the life!
[34] Accession traditionally dated 660 BC.

There is a "Mirror Rock" like the long-lost mirror rock of Senkōji. I know of one more mirror rock on an island in the Seto Inland Sea. A sign board says that a "glowing ball" was fitted into the hole, its light to be reflected by the "mirror" of highly polished rock, as some sort of "optical communication device." Something like Napoleon's semaphore telegraph?

There is an "Azimuth Rock," oriented to the four points of the compass. A vertical cleft in the rock coincides with the summer solstice sunrise.

Behind the Azimuth Rock, the "Lion Rock" faces the *winter* solstice *sunset*.

There is the "Drum Rock," carved so that it sounds like a drum or gong when struck.

Nearby is the "Birth Rock." It is a long boulder cleft in two lengthwise. The Japanese see in it the splayed legs of a woman in labour.

This whole area appears to be guarded by a huge "Falcon Rock."

The very tip-top summit of Mount Hiba is knobbed with strange bulbous rock protrusions. No sign boards draw your attention to them. They may or may not be natural. *I* have never seen anything like them. I suspect that these are even older megaliths, worn down to nubs.

THE IMPERIAL MAUSOLEUM OF IZANAMI

A huge block of a boulder lies on its side. It is half grown over with moss, and slowly sinking into the earth. Unless someone pointed it out to you, you might not even see it. But this is a very important stone. It belongs to the Emperor. According to the property list of the imperial household, this rough boulder is a "tomb" or "mausoleum." But whose?

Her name is *Izanami no Mikoto*, or *Izanami* for short. Her name means "she who invites." Izanami and her husband, Izanagi ("he who invites") are the two primordial Shinto deities, said to have given birth to the Japanese islands, and the other Shinto gods.

Yes, of the 18,032 named mountains in Japan, the Mother Goddess is buried—no, not on Mount Fuji. Not on any of the other 3,000+ meter peaks. Not where she might encourage a nearby warlord or emperor or shōgun. But out here in the boonies, on humble little round-humped Mount Hiba, *also* eponymous home of the Hibagon. Anyone want to calculate the odds of that?

Izanami's story was written down, from oral tradition, in the *Nihon Shoki*, published AD 720, the *Kojiki*, written between AD 708 and 714 by an official of the Empress Gemmyo, and the *Kogoshui*, from AD 807. Here it is.

One day, the gods Izanami and Izanagi stirred the ocean with a jewel-encrusted spear. Salt fell from the spear and turned into islands. The pair built a house on the first island, and had a wedding ceremony. During the ceremony, however, Izanami wrongly spoke before her husband. As a consequence, their first child was born an ugly boneless misshapen thing. Their second child was also unsatisfactory. The couple repeated their wedding ceremony, this time making sure that Izanagi spoke first. This lifted the curse. The couple then had auspicious offspring, including the eight principal islands of Japan, and over 800 junior gods. Then came the baby god of fire, who caused fatal burns to Izanami's vagina and genitals. She managed to give birth to three more gods: the gods of urine, feces, and vomit, which hastened her demise. She died. In revenge, Izanagi drew his sword and cut his fire-god baby son to pieces. Izanagi went down to the underworld. Izanami rashly followed. Unfortunately he was too late. Izanami had already eaten the food of the underworld, making her dead forever. Izanagi forced his way into her chamber, and—horror! His beloved was a decomposing corpse. Izanami, furious at being seen in this condition, sent the Eight Thunders and the Ugly Hags to torture her husband. Izanagi outran them, made it to the outside world, and blocked the entrance to hell with an enormous stone. Izanami is still down there, eternally angry, humiliated, and disgusted with her ever decomposing corpse-body. End.

The character 婆 in Mount Hiba (比婆山) means *hag*. Probably something to do with those Ugly Hags in the story. But please remember that the *ouni* or *wauwau* are specifically described as giant hairy mountain-dwellers with ear-to-ear mouths and the faces of *hags*.

HAUNTED CAVES

The mountain is riddled with caves. Legends say these caves are haunted by hibagon and other evil spirits. I believe these legends are correct. Read again those Shinto and Buddhist texts telling of oni living in caves. The North American bigfoot is reported to live in caves.[35] I can't help but remember the massacre of Lovelock Cave. The story is in Sarah Winnemucca Hopkins' *Life Among the Paiutes: Their Wrongs and Claims.*[36] Hopkins' Paiute ancestors were at war with a tribe of hairy cannibalistic giants. They chased them into this cave, and burned/smoked them to death.

MISSING PERSONS

Hiroshima Prefecture has a high rate of missing persons generally (2nd-highest in Japan), but it has its own clusters and hot spots. One is the mountains of Mihara. Another is in the mountains of Otake. Another is Mount Hiba.

Mihara has a population of 96,494. It is 145 times smaller than Tokyo. Tokyo has zero cases on the NPA list of mysteriously missing persons. Mihara has 3, for a case rate of 3.109. (National average: 0.264).

---

[35] See J.W. Burns' excellent article, "Introducing B.C.'s Hairy Giants" in Maclean's magazine, April 1, 1929. "Old Indians who were present said: the wild man was no doubt a "Sasquatch," a tribe of hairy people whom they claim have always lived in the mountains—in tunnels and caves."

[36] 1882. The author was the daughter of a Paiute chief.

Little Otake (pop. 27,384), is 511 times smaller than Tokyo, but it managed to get 2 cases on the NPA list, for a whopping case rate of 7.303.

The NPA list is only the tip of the iceberg. At Mihara City Hall I found 17 more people missing. At Otake City Hall I found 4 more. All but one appear to fit the same profile, including weather and wind conditions.

Mount Hiba has at least two cases of mysteriously missing people. I don't know how to calculate the rate of that because Mount Hiba has no permanent population. Searching for missing persons on Mt Fuji gives me only one case, despite Fuji being much larger, much more challenging, and much, much more visited. Mount Daisen, just over from here in Tottori, is the highest and most popular peak in the Chūgoku range. Tottori Police record 49 calls for persons going missing on that mountain in the past three years, and guess what. They found every one of them. Good for the Tottori Police. Hiroshima Police are just as good. Mount Daisen doesn't just swallow people. Mount Hiba does.

In August, 2018, a 42-year-old man went hiking alone on Mount Hiba. He has never been found. Readers of David Paulides, or anyone with outdoor experience or common sense will know that this shouldn't be. Mount Hiba is not very big. It is not especially perilous. I have been all over it and up it with my kids.

Someone might go off trail and break a leg, yes. Dogs will find them. Someone might fall off a cliff, yes. Dogs will find them. *You* could find him. Recall

Lazarus in the Bible. "He stinketh." Helicopters and drones would find them. Someone might get attacked by a bear, okay. Where's the blood and remains? Bears don't eat people cartoon like, whole: clothes, shoes, knapsacks, and all. Police with dogs, the Japanese Self-Defence Forces, and dozens of volunteers combed that mountain. They found nothing.

July 26, 2020, a 70-year-old man was participating in a climbing event on Mount Hiba. The event was slow to get going, and our man got impatient. He took off by himself, bad idea, at 9:40 AM. It was an overcast day, and rain was approaching.

No one saw the man on the mountain that whole day. By 8:30 PM he had still not returned. Over 70 people, including prefectural police, the fire brigade, and volunteers from the hiking community searched for the man for 10 days. Where did he go? Did the earth just swallow him up? Or something under the earth? I have seen mouths of caves that don't look entirely natural to me, but what do I know, I'm not a speleologist.

    Maybe one of our super tough-guy skeptics wouldn't mind sticking his head in there. Because there's no such thing as a hibagon, right?

Both men were fit. Both were happy, well-adjusted family men. Both were skinny and light. And now a word on this victim selection. The police classify people by 5 body types: Skinny, Thin, Medium, Overweight, and Fat. Of Hiroshima's 26 NPA missing cases, 7 are Skinny, 8 are Thin, and 10 are Medium. This is statistically impossible. In a country where one third of the population is overweight, we ought to have 8 overweight people, maybe more. Thin people are nimbler. We fatties (I include myself) are more likely to lose our balance and fall down a hibagon hole. There is only 1 Overweight missing person in Hiroshima, and he didn't make the cut for the NPA list. Zero Fat missing persons.

GEOLOGICAL ANOMALIES

There is a place on Mount Hiba where your compass doesn't work. Or rather it works backwards. The needle points south instead of north. Might be something to do with a rare basalt formation, might be something to do with that portal to hell. I don't know, I'm not a magnetologist.

VIRGIN FOREST

Mount Hiba is "curated" by the Hibayama Kumano Shrine. For well over a thousand years, Shinto priests have sort of hijacked and worshipped these stones and trees. One consequence from this is that *this* mountain, unlike all of the mountains around it, has never been logged. This makes Mount Hiba a highly logical sanctuary for highly intelligent wildlife.

Mount Hiba is beautiful. It has the greatest beech forests anywhere in Japan. Yew and cedar trees a hundred feet tall, and a thousand years old. You should see it. But do NOT go alone.

Remember that lady in Connecticut in 2009 who got her hands, nose, eyes, lips, and mid-face bone structure ripped off and eaten by her friend's pet chimpanzee?[37] Yeah. That was an eldely, obese, sedated animal.

Okay, now a really big chimp might stand 1.6 meters or 5'3". That's a medium-sized hibagon. The subject in our cadaver photos stood 2 meters, or 6 and a half feet, and was built like a fridge. A hibagon in the wild is not obese, and not drug-addled. He is an expert hunter with superhuman strength, stealth, speed, senses, patience, endurance, and cunning. He is also amazingly disciplined and obeys his own rules. That's why you don't hike alone. Unless you're fat like me, then you're honestly probably fine.

---

[37] Travis was a model chimp for 13 years. He had an acting and modelling career, and a happy homelife. He dressed himself, ate at the dinner table with the rest of the family, and drank wine from a stemmed wine glass. He used a computer. He mastered the TV remote control, and the Water Pik. He was a baseball fan. He bathed and slept with his owner. He was as civilized as you could expect a chimp to be. At this time in his life, Travis was morbidly obese and sedated on painkillers. Not at peak physical fitness. The face-eating rage was triggered when a visitor touched his Tickle Me Elmo doll.

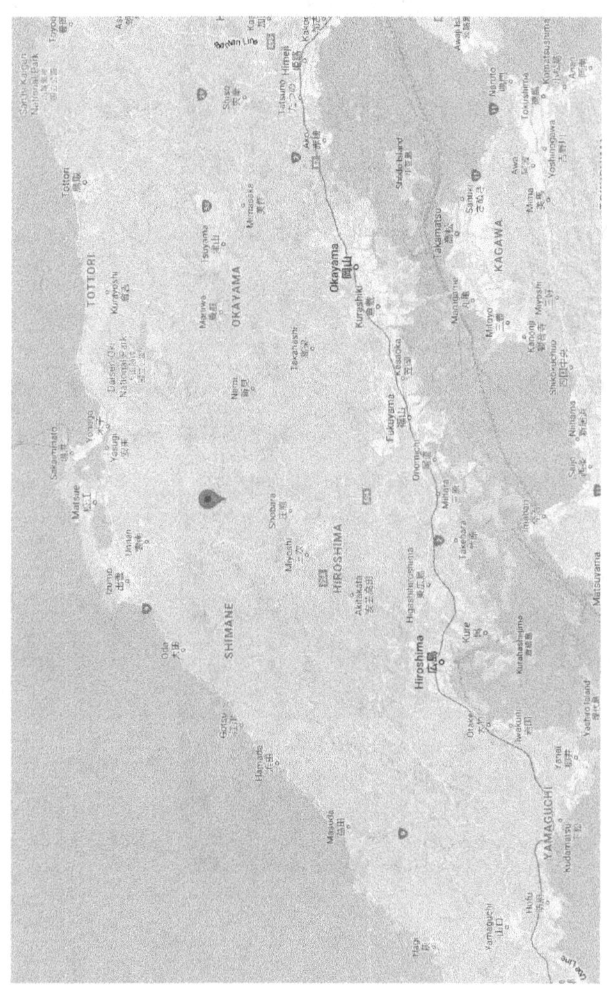

Mount Hiba, Western Japan

Mount Hiba

8 CHASING THE PHANTOM MONSTER OF MOUNT HIBA

I wanted to make a master list of Hibagon sightings. I looked through books, newspaper articles, websites, etc. in English and Japanese. What a slog! Maybe a dozen encounters came with identifying details. For the rest, you never knew if these were five different sightings, or five garbled accounts of the same sighting.

- "A Saijo man saw the beast behind his house"
- "A Saijo farmer saw the beast in his yard"
- "A Saijo man saw the beast in a field."
- "The beast was spotted in a garden behind the home of a family in Saijo."
- "Another Saijo resident spied the beast from his kitchen window."

Five or one? Do you really have (as one newspaper claims) 103 separate sightings? Or do they all boil down to half a dozen? It made me want to pull out my hair. Maybe Shobara City Hall could help? Nope. They could not.

Then I made a great discovery. There was already a (partial) master list. Saijo Yuki Town Hall published it in 1974 or 1975. It was hard to track down a copy of this pamphlet, but I did it. This document became my primary source.

"Hibayama no maboroshi no kaibutsu o otte," is the title. "Chasing the Phantom Monster of Mount Hiba" It was put out jointly by Saijo Yuki Town Hall's Promotion Division, and its Office of the Ape Clerk. The document is undated, but it was printed late in 1974 or early in 1975. The last sighting in the document is from August 15, 1974, and the Office of the Ape Clerk was abolished in March, 1975.

It lists 29 separate, dated sightings. Some of these include multiple witnesses, so the 29 sightings involve at least 34 eyewitnesses. Plus an unknown number of persons from local police, a university survey team, and a troop of boy scouts. The document gives places, dates, and a few witness comments. Each sighting has the initials of the eyewitness or, in the case of a group, a chief eyewitness. When you go through *my* list of sightings, you can tell which ones come from this document because they have witnesses' initials.

My list also has sightings after "Chasing the Phantom Monster of Mount Hiba;" sightings not included by the Ape Clerk; and the now confirmed first sighting, the children's mushroom-picking sighting. Here now is the most comprehensive list of separate Hibagon sightings. But first, this word from the Ape Clerk:

A WORD FROM THE APE CLERK

Human or monkey? The mysterious monster of Mount Hiba (now known as the Hibagon), which appeared in July of 1970 and has become a hot topic, is more credible thanks to his many witnesses. As a result, the facts are becoming gradually more established. In April of 1971, an ape clerk was assigned to work on witness records, information gathering, etc., but we have not been able to respond satisfactorily to all inquiries from various fields and requests for materials. We apologize for the inconvenience, for which we are heartily embarrassed. Finally, I would like to summarize the frenzy here, report it to everyone, and present to you the unique and humorous monster "Hibagon." In this murderous modern society, we hope that you will cherish a simple and romantic dream, and that it will be the basis for the recovery of even a little of the humanity that has been lost.[38]
[Signed] APE CLERK

---

[38] Written 30 years after the atomic bombing of Hiroshima City, and only 100 km away.

怪物出没状況一覧表

	目撃日時	場所	怪獣の状態	足跡など	目撃者（当時の年齢）敬称略
1	45・7・20 20	西城町油木衣木ダム附近	ゴリラに似て子牛ぐらい。	水にぬれた足跡。泥水踏み倒される。	西城町　[illegible]（31）
2	7・23 5	同　自宅附近畑	異様な顔。人間に近い。	草がなぎ倒されていた。	同　[illegible]（43）
3	7・30 20	油木自宅附近	1.6m。顔に毛がはえ逆三角形。剛毛。		同　[illegible]（47）
4	8・30 19	同　農道	子牛のように四つんばい。ゴリラのよう。		同　[illegible]（43）
5	9・3 8	同　大田ヶ原	茶かっ色の毛をした大猿のよう。	トウモロコシが30本なぎ倒される。	同　[illegible]（47）
6	10・8 朝	同　農兵の森		足跡1・2個。縦14、幅7cm	同　[illegible]（50）ら2人
7	10・12 15	同　湯之原	子牛のよう。茶かっ色。額は仙。胴長		同　[illegible]（67）
8	7・9 15	同　三井野原第1踏切	全身茶色の毛。前かがみ。1.8m。出歯。		岡山県津山市・[illegible]（55）
9	11・20 朝	西城町下尺迫境野川沿い		わぐらか。トウモロコシの食べカス多量。	西城町役所　[illegible]（49）
10	11・11 20	東城町小奴可持丸自宅附近	全身黒毛。体を左右にゆする。		東城町　[illegible]（80）
11	11・13 6	小奴可	全身黒毛。大猿のよう。		同　[illegible]（38）
12	12・16 10	比和町吾妻山池の原		足跡7個。皆で変形。縦21、幅22cm	松江市黒田町　[illegible]（22）
13	46・3・21 夜	西城町宣帽子山中		足跡300m点々。縦24、幅10cm	島根県仁多郡　[illegible]（80）
14	9・3 18	同油木戻庭自宅附近	山掟の木上、1.5〜1.6m。大猿の2倍。		西城町　[illegible]（53）
15	46・9・4 10	岡中戦発電所山頂附近		足跡4個。縦24、幅23cm	庄原市　[illegible]（45）
16	9・7 14	同県民の森鳥帽子山林道		足跡37個。縦18、幅13cm	同　[illegible]（45）
17	9・14 17	同中野大風呂山山中	1.5〜1.6m。茶かっ色。顔逆三角形。		西城町　[illegible]（13）
18	10・24 夜	同県民の森鳥帽子山林道		足跡6個。縦18、幅13cm	名城大調査隊　[illegible]ほか
19	12・15 16	岡比婆山駅北側煙道山山中	1.5mくらい。全身黒毛。歩き方ゴリラのよう	爪跡あり6カ所。	同　[illegible]（69）
20	47・4・2 朝	岡油木衣木山中		足跡点々。縦18、幅13cm	京都市　[illegible]（15）
21	5・24 13	岡山中国道上7カ所	1.5m。黒っぽい毛に覆われ横歩き。		島根県仁多郡　[illegible]（41）
22	8・14 朝	同県民の森看板より1,500m雑木林の中	足跡	足跡多数。縦25、幅15cm	神戸市ボーイスカウト隊　[illegible]（23）
23	11・7 12	比和町三河内山ろく	ゴリラのよう。黒毛に覆われ目口が大きい。	雑木が踏み倒される。	比和町　[illegible]（26）
24	11・29 7	同町山川林道	足跡	足跡700m点々と。縦16、幅10〜12cm	同　[illegible]（35）
25	48・2・3 18	同三河内一本松	二本足で歩く。全身濃茶色の毛。		同　[illegible]（54）ら3人
26	4・23 11	西城町油木国道314号線上	身体を左右にゆすり歩く。体長1.5m		西城町　[illegible]（42）
27	49・6・20 10	庄原市川北町頬川県道上	全身茶色。剛毛、1.5mゴリラに似ている。		高野町　[illegible]（33）
28	7・15	比和町森脇の県道	大猿が四つんばい、1.5m。全身茶色。		比和町　[illegible]（65）
29	8・15	庄原市高川町大谷内戸ノ丸山国有林そばの県道	写真撮影成功。		同　[illegible]（41）

発刊にあたって

〝人間かサルか〟昭和45年7月に出没して話題となった比婆山の謎の怪物（現在ではヒバゴンとよばれ親しまれている）も多数の目撃者によりその実在はより信憑性がましてきました。

　昭和46年4月類人猿係が置かれ、目撃記録、情報の収集、等々の仕事を務としてまいりましたが各方面からのお問い合せや、資料提供の要望に今まで満足にお答えすることが出来ず大変ご迷惑をおかけしたことと存じます。

やっとここに経過を集約して、皆さんにご報告すると共にユニークでユーモラスな怪物「ヒバゴン」を推進してみたいと思います。

　殺伐とした現代社会その中で素朴でロマネスクな夢をほのぼのと育てていただき、少しでも失なわれる人間性回復のよりどころとなりえれば幸甚に存じます。

類人猿係

The Message from the Ape Clerk

9 THE SIGHTINGS

Spring or early summer, 1970: Elementary school students are picking mushrooms on Mount Hiba. An ape-like creature crashes through nearby bushes. The children run home. No one believes them.

July 20, 1970: Three town employees from Saijo Yuki are riding in the cab of a public utilities truck. They are on Route 314. They pull onto the road that runs past the Rokunohara Dam.[39] They drive west on this road. As they come around the bend at the head of the dam, they see a creature come out of the woods on the north side.[40] The driver stops on the large curved shoulder beside the dam.[41] The creature crosses the road approximately 90 meters ahead. It walks west along the reservoir and the Rokunohara River about 230 meters until the river narrows. Then it crosses the river and goes up into the woods on the south side. The men watch until they lose it among the trees.

---

[39] We have precise locations for these first three sightings, so I encourage everyone to follow along on Google Maps. Searching "Rokunohara Dam" will take you right there.

[40] You can see a large rock face on the north side of the road, across from the dam. At the western edge of this rock face there is a gully. This is where Hibagon came out onto the road.

[41] Reminder: Japanese drive on the left side of the road.

After the creature is gone, the men get out of the truck to look around. They find muddy footprints "filled with water." "Miscellaneous trees were trampled."[42] Getting back in the truck, they drive into Saijo Yuki and report their sighting. They say that the creature walked erect on two legs. It looked "like a gorilla," and was "about the size of a calf."[43] One of the men, initials Y.M., aged 31, signs the report.

Y.M. was probably the eldest. So we have three men in their physical prime. Working men. Area natives. They know the land. They know the fauna. This is a daytime encounter at 90 meters. Misidentification can be ruled out. Hoax can also be ruled out. These are men on government jobs, on government time. Would all three agree to risk their names, reputations, jobs, livelihoods, families, and futures...for what? For a hoax? Recall, bigfoot is unknown in Japan at this time (and even today).

July 23, 1970. Zoom out from the Rokunohara Dam, and continue west along the Rokunohara River road. You will see a large, polygonal rice paddy. The road curves up north and west around this paddy. Just where the road starts to curve up, look straight west across the pond. Two houses are close together. The southern one has a black roof,

---

[42] Snapped branches? Trees pushed over? I wish we had more details.
[43] Calves have an average birth weight of 86 lbs (39 kg), and an average weaning weight of 600 lbs (272 kg).

and the northern one has a brown roof.[44] It was
back behind the brown-roofed house, up the slope,
and into the treeline that the creature was spotted
again.

The witness was a 43-year-old farmer and lifelong
resident with the initials M.K. I don't know where
M.K. was standing, but the farthest away he could
have been, and still had a line of sight to the
creature, was inside his house. From M.K.'s back
windows to the treeline it is 70-100 meters (76-109
yards).[45] The creature came out of these woods
into M.K.'s back field.

M.K. said that the creature had a "strange,
grotesque" face, with "piercing, intelligent eyes." He
felt that the creature was "close to human." When
he looked behind his house later, M.K. found
places where the grass was "beaten down."[46]

July 30, 1970: Go north from M.K.'s house about 2
kilometers (1.24 miles). You come to two brown-
tiled farm houses, just where this road becomes
Route 256.

Farmer S.I., 47 years old, is out between two
fields. A black gorilla-like creature comes down the
hill, out of the forest, and proceeds to walk toward
him. S.I. estimates its height at 1.6 meters (5'3"). Its
head is disproportionately large. Its face is like an

---

[44] As of 2021, Google Maps.
[45] The treeline is not straight.
[46] A track? A nesting bed?

"inverted triangle," and hairy with "bristles." It sways from side to side. It is unhurried.

  S.I. runs back to his house. Runs inside, and tells his family to lock all the doors and windows. Then he goes out and hops in his car. He drives the 40 meters (130 feet) to his cousin's house, to warn him. No one ever saw S.I. so upset.

August 30, 1970: Witness S.T., 43 years old, sees Hibagon (as he is now called) on a Prefectural road. It is "like a gorilla."

September 3, 1970: Witness M.T., 47 years old, sees Hibagon. "Like a large monkey with brown hair." Reports 30 corn stalks knocked down.[47]

October 8, 1970: Witness I.N., 50 years old, and two other witnesses see Hibagon in prefectural forest. They investigate and find one or two footprints, 14 x 7 centimeters (5.5" x 2.25").

October 12, 1970: Witness T.S., 67 years old, sees Hibagon at Yunohara. The creature is big "like a calf, but the face is a monkey."

November 9, 1970: Witness J.M., 55 years old, sees Hibagon at the Miinohara No. 1 railroad crossing. Reports that the creature's body is all covered with brown hair. Height is estimated at 1.8 meters (5'9"). Hibagon has an overbite.[48]

---

[47] I wonder if the corn was taken or not.

November 11, 1970: Witness M.H., 86 years old, sees Hibagon outside his/her house in Tojo village, some 25 km southeast of Mount Hiba. (Hibayama Station is between the two points, 15 km northwest of Tojo. Tojo is also connected to the Geibi train line. This is important in relation to the December 15, 1971 sighting.) The creature's body was covered in black hair. It swayed from side to side.

November 13, 1970: Witness T.W., 38 years old, sees Hibagon in Onuka ward, Shobara City. This is a more built-up area with a post office, a train station, a few shops, etc. T.W. says the creature's whole body was black and hairy, and it looked like a big monkey.

November 20, 1970: Anonymous employee of Saijocho Bessho High School, 49 years old, sees Hibagon walking along the Kumano River in Shimosakuda, Saijo Yuki. Notes a large amount of corn destroyed nearby. Witness wonders if the creature made his "roost" in the corn.

December 16, 1970: Witness Y.S., 22 years old, finds Hibagon's bare footprints in the snow near Hiwacho Azumayama Pond, behind a secluded lodge resort-style hotel 3 km (1.8 miles) west of

---

[48] Fascinating detail. Please remember this when we come to the cadaver photos.

Mount Hiba. The footprints, "deformed by snow," measure 21 cm (length) by 22 cm (width).

December, 1970 (day unknown): A troop of boy scouts finds footprints in the snow on Mt. Azuma, near the December 16th footprint sighting. The barefoot prints measure 21 centimeters (8.25 inches) and the track stretches 300 meters (984 feet).

[NOTE: I have *read* that there were twelve separate Hibagon sightings reported in December, 1970. I can find identifiable details for only two.]

March 21, 1971: Witness K.K., 48 years old, finds Hibagon footprints in a Saijo Yuki municipal yard. Footprints measure 24x10 cm and form a 300m track.

April, 1971: Saijo Yuki Town Hall creates Office of the Ape Clerk. Duties to include: [1] Information collection and recording. Upon receiving news of sightings or findings of footprints, the Ape Clerk will rush to the site to collect information and record witnesses' statements. In some cases, a detailed examination of the area will result in the discovery of more footprints by the Ape Clerk himself. [2] Media support. The Ape Clerk will respond to the media, and supply local information. [3] Inquiry window. The Ape Clerk will take written inquiries and telephone calls from all over the country. [4] Survey team assistance. The Office of the Ape

Clerk will help to organize, and in some cases subsidize, university expeditions and survey teams from all over Japan. [5] "Nuisance fee" payments. The Ape Clerk will pay "nuisance fees" (up to 5,000 yen) to local witnesses with good claims that their work, income, routine, quality of life, privacy, property, or other important concerns have been hurt by media attention, trespassers, etc.

September 3, 1971: Witness T.F., 53 years old, sees Hibagon spotted outside his/her home in Jinseki.[49] The creature is loitering around a mountain cherry tree. T.F. estimates its height at 1.5 to 1.6 meters.

September 4, 1971: Witness T.T., 45 years old, finds four Hibagon footprints near the Chubu Electric Power Station. The footprints are 24cm (length) by 23cm (width).

September 7, 1971: Witness Y.S., 45 years old, finds a track of 37 footprints, 18x13cm. Found on a prefectural road (probably Route 254) on Tateeboshiyama, approx. 1.8 km southwest of Mount Hiba.

---

[49] A good 30 km south-southeast from the Rokunohara Dam, and forested mountains all the way. Shows the range and/or distribution of the hibagon. My wife's parents' farm is here in Jinseki. Many relatives are here. I know the area well.

September 14, 1971: Witness K.M., 13 years old, sees Hibagon outside a hot spring public bath[50] The creature is brown, and approx. 1.6 meters tall.

October 24, 1971: Witness Y.S., 45 years old, finds a track of 37 footprints measuring 18cm (length) by 13cm (width). Tracks are found in a prefectural forest. Y.S. is part of a survey team from Meijo University, Nagoya.

December 15, 1971: Witness R.N., 69 years old, sees Hibagon north of Hibayama Station, on the Geibi train line, 7 km almost due south from the Rokunohara Dam. This stretch of track runs north-south. On the west side, you have unbroken forested mountains all the way back to Mount Hiba. R.N. estimates the creature to be 1.5 meters tall, and covered in black hair. It walks like a gorilla. The report notes "six places with claw marks," which *I* guess were not claws as such, but overgrown toenails.

April 2, 1972: Witness S.K., 16 years old, finds footprints in Yuki village, Jinseki. Prints measure 18 cm long, and 13 cm wide.

May 24, 1972: Witness M.M., 41 years old, sees Hibagon on the side of a mountain, again in Jinseki.

---

[50] Hibagon drawn by lady bathers? The witness K.M. was small and light. She could have barely missed becoming an abductee. K.M, if you are still out there, please contact me. I want to know more.

The creature is described as 1.6 meters, covered with dark hair, and walking sideways.[51]

Summer, 1972: Kobe University research team investigates, and determines that Hibagon (whatever it is) is real.[52] Police make plaster casts of footprints found at a construction site.

August 14, 1972: Witness T.K., 23 years old, is the leader of a Kobe City boy scout corps visiting the area. The scouts find many footprints 1.5 km into a prefectural forest. Prints measure 25 cm by 15 cm.

November 7, 1972: Witness R.I., 26 years old, sees Hibagon in Hiwacho Mitsugaichi, a village on the western slope of Mount Hiba. (See December 16, 1970.) He reports that the creature looks something like a gorilla. It is covered in black hair. It has black eyes. It was trampling trees.[53]

---

[51] Travelling sideways? Stepping sideways into cover?
[52] They cited the excellent quality of the eyewitness testimony, and the genuine, inimitable fear displayed by the eyewitnesses. Kobe University is currently ranked #15 in Japan [Times Higher Education: The World University Rankings]. For reference, the US university currently ranked #15 is Columbia [Wall Street Journal/Times Higher Education College Rankings 2020].
[53] Multiple reports of beating down grass, knocking down corn, and trampling trees. Territorial displays? Displays of strength? Directional signs? Bedding?

November 29, 1972: Witness T.I., 35 years old, finds footprints on a Yamakawa forest road, east of Mount Hiba, near the Rokunohara River. The track extends 700 meters (765 yards). The prints are 16 cm by 12 cm.

February 3, 1973: Witness M.K. 54 years old, together with three other witnesses, see Hibagon in a place called Mikawachi Ipponmatsu (三河内一本松).[54] The creature was walking on two legs. It was covered in long brown hair. The witnesses said it was thin.

April 23, 1973: Witness N.K., 42 years old, sees Hibagon in Saijo Yuki by Route 314. The creature was swaying from side to side. Estimates its height at 1.5 meters.

June 20, 1973: Witness S.O., 33 years old, sees Hibagon in Kawagitacho, a small farming hollow outside of Shobara City. The creature looked like a gorilla. It was covered in brown hair. It was approximately 1.6 meters tall.

June 20, 1974: Anonymous motorist describes Hibagon walking along and across a road in a series of hopping leaps.

---

[54] I have not been able to locate it. Looks like a company name. Probably now defunct.

July 15, 1974: Witness K.H. sees Hibagon on a prefectural road in Hiwacho, near his/her house. K.H. describes it as very apelike, and walking on all fours. Brown. 1.6 meters.

August 15, 1974: Witness Y.M., 41 years old, is driving his car in, again, Hiwacho. He sees a large, black animal walking on all fours beside the road. When the creature hears the car, it stands up and walks into the trees. The driver stops and snaps a photo of the creature trying to hide behind a persimmon tree. It is a blobsquatch, but thank you, Y.M., for trying.

August 18, 1974: A man sees the monster in Shobara. The creature is "man height," but the torso is "twice as thick as a man's."

October 11, 1974: Last sighting for a while.

March, 1975: Saijo Yuki Town Hall Office of the Ape Clerk is abolished; the clerk is reassigned.

1980: Hibagon is seen "fleeing" across a river, with a "bounding gait" in the village of Yamano, some 50 km (30 miles) southeast of Mount Hiba, and tantalizingly close (16 km) to my own house.

1981: Again spotted in Yamano, outside of a health centre.

1982: Hibagon is spotted in Mitsugi, some 30 km west of Yamano, and roughly 60 km (37 miles) due south of Mount Hiba. All of these areas (Mount Hiba, Shobara, Saijo, Yamano, Mitsugi) are connected by dense forest. Hibagon was estimated now to be 2 meters (6'5") tall, and carrying a stone tool, "like an axe." The only, very precious, report of Hibagon carrying an alleged tool or weapon, like an oni. This is the last reported sighting of Hibagon.

  These are all of the sightings I could find. As to the credibility of the eyewitnesses, here is Egi Katsuyuki, Ape Clerk:

"They were above lying, I can tell you that."[55]

---

[55] Asahi Shimbun newspaper article, August 13, 2020: "Japan's 'Bigfoot' still influences Hiroshima town after 50 years."

Rokunohara Dam
Rokunohara River
Rokunohara River
July 20, 1970 Sighting

July 23, 1970
Rokunohara River
Rokunohara River
Rokunohara River
Rokunohara Dam
六の原ダム

256
比婆山県民の森線
比婆山県民の森線
比婆山県民の森線
Rokunohara River
Rokunohara River
July 30, 1970

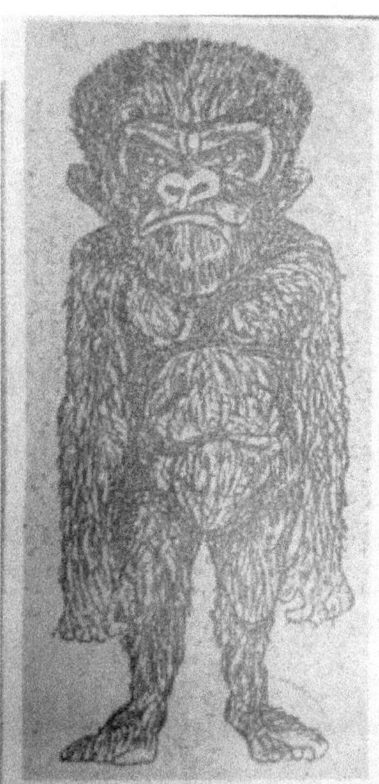

当時の中国新聞に載ったヒバゴンのイメージイラスト（1970年10月15日付）

31歳だった目撃者の男性から、後日、直接聞いた話だという。

■相次ぐ目撃談

同年7月～74年8月の間、西城町を中心に、現在の庄原市北部で目撃や足跡の発見が相次いだ。

色の剛毛が立つ。体も同系色の荒々しい毛で覆われているとの姿が浮かび上がってきた。

ヒバゴンが、世間に知られるきっかけになったのは70年8月26日の中国新聞の記事だった。「比婆山山ろくで、あぜ道を歩いてく

自宅近くで草刈りをしていたところ、人間の顔立ちに似た動物が、草むらから上半身を出して突っ立っていた。

30日の現場は、さらに2㌔離れた水田。47歳の男性が午後8時ころ、

Persimmon tree photo from Y.M.

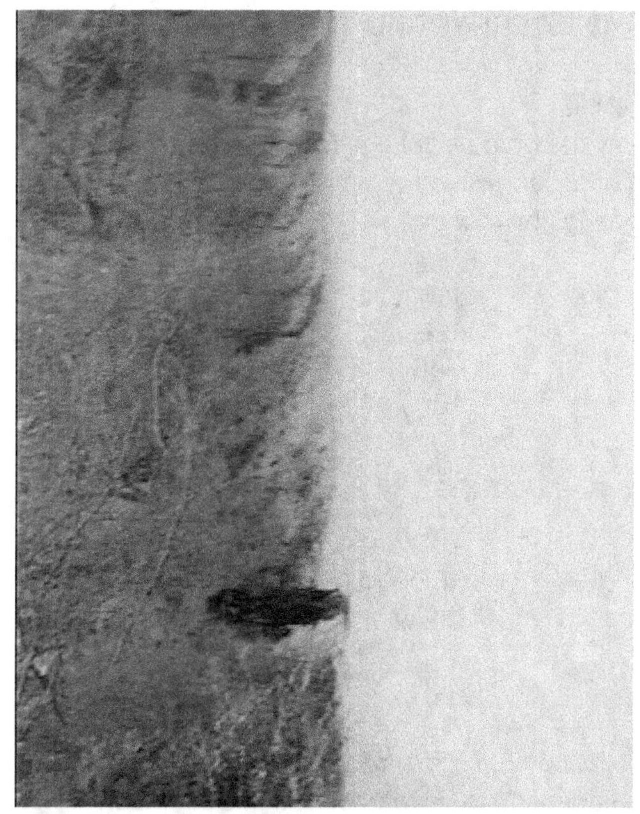

Walking in snow photo (source unknown)

10 INTERPRETING THE DATA

SEASONALITY

Taking only the *dated* sightings (day, month, year), a pattern of seasonality emerges. Here are the dated sightings by month:

JAN	0
FEB	1
MAR	2
APR	3
MAY	1
JUN	2
JUL	4
AUG	4
SEPT	5
OCT	4
NOV	6
DEC	3

I am not including, for example, the twelve sightings supposed to have occurred in December, 1970. For that month we have only two *dated* sightings. We must hope that the reported, dated sightings are somehow proportional to the frequency of all sightings.

November is the most active month, with Sept-Nov being the busiest 3-month block. This suggests a bear-like autumnal hyperphagia. July-Sept is another busy block, coinciding with the harvests of many crops.

AGGRESSION

Hibagon is non-aggressive *in this record of encounters*. Some of our missing persons, were they not ipso facto involuntarily absent, might care to disagree. But *in the testimony of surviving eyewitnesses* we must give this to the Hibagon: he terrifies eyewitnesses, but is never violent. He commits no theft or property damage, beyond knocking down some corn stalks.[56]

HOWEVER: Old reports of hibagon by other names tell of abduction, rape, and predation. He stalks. He ambushes. He flushes. He encircles. He mimics. He comes up through your toilet.

SIZE

Hibagon's average height is 160cm, the same as the *kakusaru* or *jueyuan* of Gifu Prefecture. The subject of the cadaver photos is approx. 2 meters tall. This matches the 1982 sighting.

SEX

Hibagon's sexual characteristics are never mentioned. Obviously, both males and females must exist. Sex is usually apparent in North American bigfoot sightings. The omission is probably due to the decorum of our eyewitnesses and the natural modesty of our young, unmarried Ape Clerk.

---

[56] I did a lot more damage than that, just helping my father-in-law on his farm. I broke his arm once, helping him move timber.

DECREASING FREQUENCY, INCREASING RANGE

Hibagon sightings decrease over time, even as his range increases. This suggests to me that he is getting more comfortable in his environment and improving his hibagon skill set.

INVESTIGATORS CONVINCED

Hibagon and the eyewitnesses convinced police and university research teams that he was real. Not a hoax. Not a case of mistaken identity. University researchers were especially impressed by [1] the footprints; [2] the witnesses' genuine fear.

CONSISTENT EYEWITNESS DESCRIPTIONS

Hibagon is described with amazing consistency. Not one account deviates in any significant way.

CONSISTENT BIGFOOT-LIKE BEHAVIOUR

Japanese eyewitnesses to hibagon, 1970-1982, knew nothing about North American bigfoot. But they reported physical and behavioural characteristics, including hiding behind trees, side-to-side swaying, and the damaging or marking of vegetation.

THE FOOTPRINTS

These deserve their own discussion.

11 THE FOOTPRINTS

The standard Hibagon narrative wants to tell you about a single individual. In "Chasing the Phantom Monster of Mount Hiba," Ape Clerk Mr Egi refers three times in the third person singular: *"the mysterious monster,"* *"the unique and humorous monster,"* and *"him."* My friends do this too. "Oh yes, *the Hibagon is* the *yōkai* of the mountain." But this is demonstrably wrong. The footprints show a group. We have 6 different sizes of footprint that must have been made by more than one hibagon. Some difference might be explained by growing feet, but let's look at them in chronological order:

- 14 cm (Oct. 1970)
- 21 cm (Dec. 1970)[57]
- 24 cm (Mar. 1971)
- 24 cm (Sep. 1971)
- 18 cm (Sep. 1971)
- 18 cm (Oct. 1971)
- 18 cm (Apr. 1972)
- 25 cm (Aug. 1972)
- 16 cm (Nov. 1972)

It is *unlikely* that a hibagon with 14 cm feet in October, 1970 will have 21 cm feet just two months

---

[57] Footprints described as "deformed," suggesting that feet smaller than 21cm made these prints. Thawing, shuffling, crumbling, slipping, etc. would all result in larger prints. More imaginatively, the subject could have backtracked. Or multiple hibagon could have stepped in a leader's tracks.

later. But it is *impossible* that a hibagon with 21 cm, 24 cm, or 25 cm feet will later have smaller feet of 18 cm or 16 cm.

Furthermore, it is unlikely that a 160 cm tall primate is going to have a 14 cm foot, or even a 16 cm or 18 cm foot. Chimps, orangutans, and gorillas all have large feet compared to humans, and relative to body weight.[58] Have a look at average body weights and feet:

Chimp	Orang.	Gorilla	Human
29 kg	47 kg	58 kg	76 kg
20 cm	26 cm	24.5 cm	26 cm

Bigfoot-type creatures also have big feet. And that is what we see in the cadaver photos: a creature with basically no ankles. His legs look like snow pants over ski boots. Here are some *human* feet, from my own family:

- Adult male: 26 cm foot, 175 cm
- Adult female: 21.5 cm foot, 157 cm
- 9-yr-old girl: 20 cm foot, 138 cm
- 4-yr-old girl: 14 cm foot, 100 cm

Human feet are small. The median hibagon height is my wife's height, whereas the median hibagon foot size is mine. So I'm looking at a creature my

---

[58] Weije Wang, et al. "Analysis of joint force and torque for the human and non-human ape foot during bipedal walking with implications for the evolution of the foot." Journal of Anatomy, 2014.

wife's size, with my size feet, i.e. big feet. Of course, bodies/feet can be scaled down for females and juveniles, and up for mature males. If my family left tracks in the mud or snow, anyone could tell that we were four individuals. A trained tracker (police, boy scout leader, university researcher, Ape Clerk) would spot that right away.

I think we have a *minimum* of five individuals. Whoever left the 24cm prints in Sept. '71 could easily have grown into 25cm feet by August of '72. But I don't see fewer than five hibagon leaving these footprints.

You might see a minimum of 4, not five. But I don't think anyone can see fewer than four. This is good news because it tells of a thriving group of different sizes, ages, and sexes. A *family* group, like my own family group. I see 3 juveniles (14cm, 16cm, 18cm) and at least two adults (21cm, 24cm, 25cm) in the group. This is the minimum. There is no maximum because:

- Every track could have been made by a different hibagon.
- There could be any number of hibagon in the group who left no tracks.

Why did the Ape Clerk promote the Lone Hibagon narrative? I don't know. But whatever the reason *then*, Mr Egi *now* believes that the hibagon are doing quite well, thank you.

"I'm blessed with six grandchildren. I believe Hibagon, too, is living peacefully somewhere deep in the mountains, surrounded by grandchildren," he said in the August 13, 2020 Asahi Shimbun article.

I hope so too, Mr Egi. I hope so too.

The footprints are all five-toed. They have a midtarsal break. Bigfoot enthusiasts will know what this means.

If you want to see hibagon plaster footprint casts, right now you can go to the Hiroshima Prefectural Police in Shobara City. They have a pair on display. They have more casts in their evidence vault. The HPP's official position is that the hibagon is real, and the footprints are real.

In 2017, Fuji TV (フジテレビ, *Fuji Terebi*) did a Hibagon segment for the May 17 episode of its popular "What's this in the World!? Mystery" series. It was supposed to be a simple retrospective. It turned out to be a major scoop.

A crew came down from Tokyo. Visited sightings locations. Interviewed relatives of witnesses, and Mr Egi the retired Ape Clerk. It was a very nice retelling of the story.

What happened to change that, as I understand it, was this. The crew had it "in the can." They were packed up and saying their goodbyes. The producer was talking with one of the locals. Their conversation went something like this.

PRODUCER: Well, thanks again for everything.
LOCAL: Thank *you* for coming and telling our story.
PRODUCER: Great story. Just too bad that it ends so suddenly. So mysteriously.
LOCAL: What do you mean?
PRODUCER: The way the sightings just stopped.
LOCAL: Well, it's no mystery, is it? He died, poor bugger.
PRODUCER: Hibagon died? You think so?
LOCAL: Well, sure we don't think so. We *know* so.
PRODUCER: How?
LOCAL: Oh. They found the body.
PRODUCER: They found the body!?

LOCAL: Oh, yes. A feller found the body. No one told you?
PRODUCER: What happened to it? Where is the body now?
LOCAL: Well, the feller and his buddies buried it.
PRODUCER: They buried the body. Where?
LOCAL: Don't know. Those fellers all passed away, and they didn't say where.
PRODUCER: So nobody knows where.
LOCAL: Nope.
PRODUCER: That's too bad.
LOCAL: Yep.
PRODUCER: Well...
LOCAL: Sure lucky they took those photos, though.
PRODUCER: Photos?
LOCAL: Sure, they took photos before they buried it.
PRODUCER: Where are the photos?
LOCAL: Think I might have some at home somewhere. Want to see them?

The local produced the photos, and Fuji TV put them in the piece. This is delightful and horrifying. How much other evidence has never been seen? How close did these photos come to being lost or destroyed? Old folks die. Their things get thrown out and incinerated.

Fuji TV is Japan's 3rd biggest network. It is a major, respected news network. Now let's finally see the photos.

Photo One, cropped

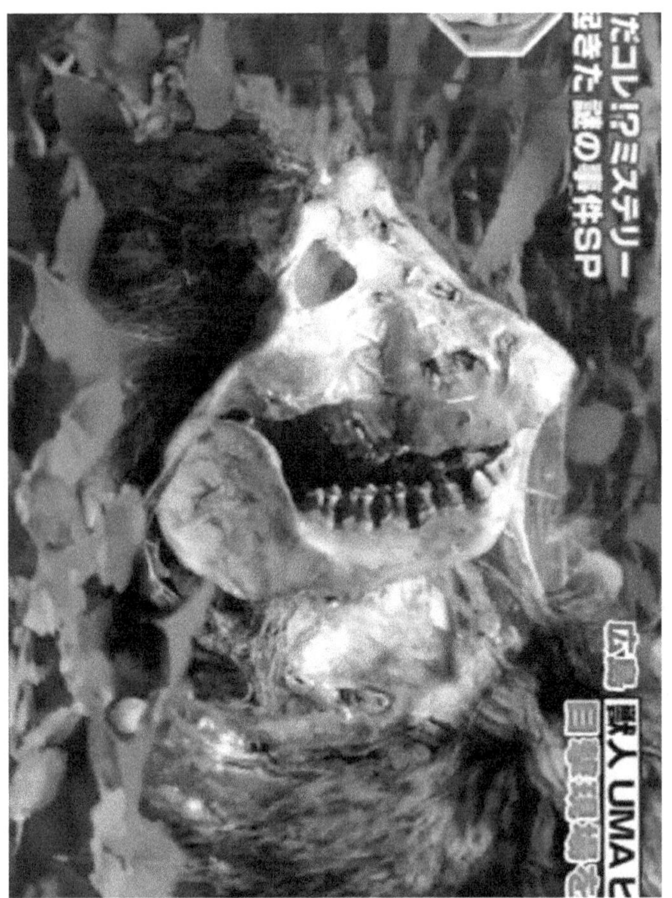

Photo Two, cropped and rotated 90°

13 THE CADAVER PHOTOS

PHOTO ONE. Hibagon lies on his back, one skeletal hand lying over his exposed spine and rib cage. If his elbow is where I think it is, and you extended that arm down, his fingers would hang lower than his knees. Our poor Hibagon looks like an empty sleeping bag or a trophy hunter's rug. Flat and deflated. Still we can see that he was a thick lad. His left leg at the calf is 2.5 times wider than the rubber boots worn by the farmer. His calf is wider than the farmer's thigh. At the waist, Hibagon is easily twice as wide as the farmer. What was the eyewitness statement? *Man-height, but torso twice as big as a man's.*[59] How much did this hibagon weigh? From his height and bulk, and extrapolating from gorilla weights, I put his living weight at 250-300 kg or 550-660 lbs.[60]

PHOTO TWO. Let's dissect it bit by bit.

LOWER JAW. The first thing we have to do, we have to replace the lower jaw. Hibagon's lower jaw

---

[59] Also, again, the description of the Mississippi Wild Man: "...about the average height of man, but of far greater muscular development." Although at 2 meters, this hibagon is rather taller than the average Japanese man.

[60] It is too bad that records of Hibagon's footprints never tell the depth. It might be possible to return to the same ground and, with dummy feet and weights, do some experiments. Original ground conditions could be recreated from meteorological data.

has fallen down and off. You know when you go to bed a little drunk? Your jaw collapses, and you snore yourself awake. At least I do. Hibagon looks like that, except he can't snore himself awake and restore his jaw because he is dead and his face is rotted away, with all of the muscles and connective tissues.

There is a curved groove in the maxilla (upper jaw). It looked to me that the forward edge of the ramus (the upward angled arm) of the mandible (lower jaw) used to fit into and slide in this groove. I asked my haematologist friend, and he said yes. The groove is where the bottom jaw was hinged. We have to return the jaw to that groove, called the coronoid process. I have outlined the groove and the coronoid process in the following photo. And then, in the next photo, I have copied the mandible and put it in the right place. My haematologist friend said, "Good." The jaw itself is huge, compared even to a gorilla or a bear. The height of the ramus increases lever arm and torque. This guy's bite force is off the scale.

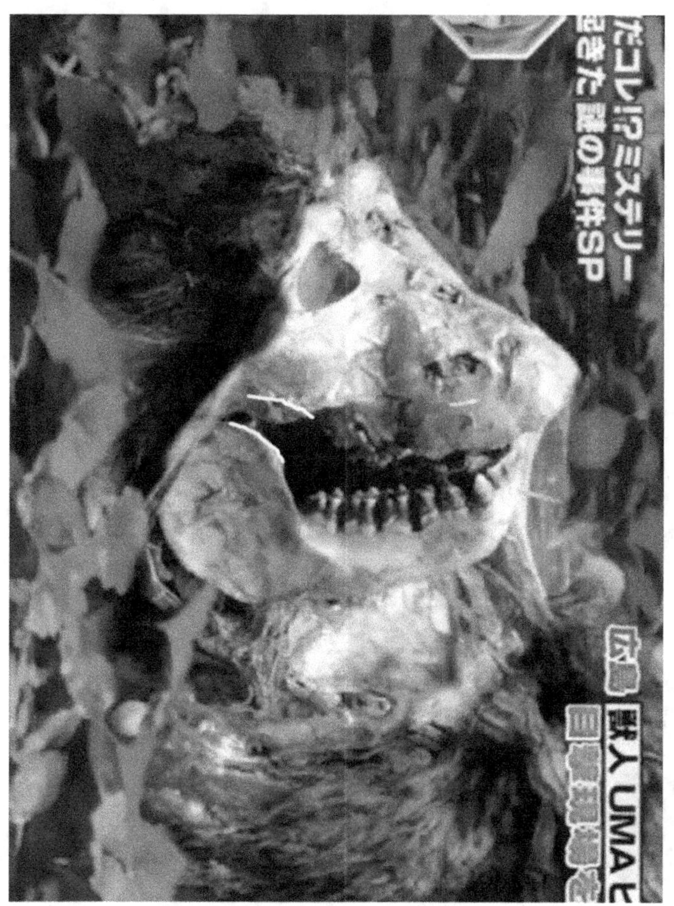

This is where the jaw should go

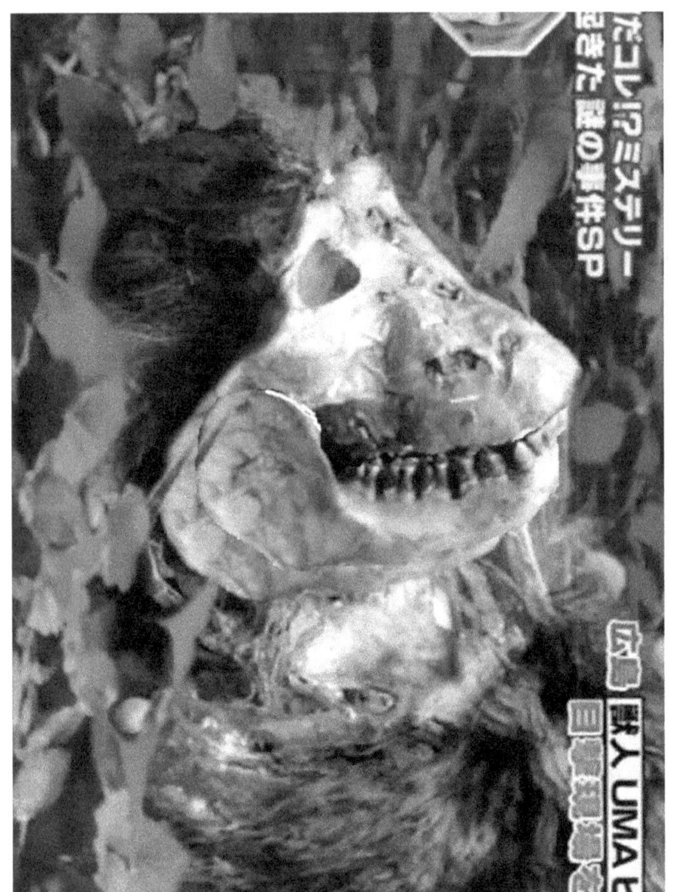

That's better!

TEETH. The bottom dentition is well preserved and human-like. Even the correct number of teeth (8) on the right mandible, the same as an adult human. Yet the uppers appear to be missing or worn. Or the camera angle is bad. Apelike large canines are notably absent.

MAXILLA: The cadaver appears to have a bony snout or muzzle. As explained above, this is the result of the displaced mandible. Put the mandible back into its proper position, and the "snout" is seen as pronounced prognathism. Recall the eyewitness who reported seeing an overbite. I think we may have a combination of facial prognathism plus alveolar prognathism (dental portion of upper jaw, a.k.a. overbite). Probably not all hibagon, or all bigfoot, will have this feature. We are looking at an individual. Humans don't look all alike. Some individual people, and some people groups, have features that others don't.[61]

---

[61] Mandibular prognathism is relatively low in American Indian populations (2.6-3.1%) but high (16%) among the Eskimo or Inuit of Labrador. Some families of bigfoot will be more prognathic, and others less. See Otero, Morford, Falcão-Alencar, and Hartsfield, "Family History and Genetics of Mandibular Prognathism," in Orthodontic Treatment of Class III Malocclusion. And Tassopoulou-Fishell, et al., "Genetic Variation in Myosin 1H Contributes to Mandibular Prognathism," American Journal of Orthodontics & Dentofacial Orthopedics, March, 2013.

NASAL APERTURE: Hard to see in this photo. We have a bad combination of detritus inside the aperture, sun glare, and a bad camera angle. Examining photos of skulls shot from similar angles, I find many examples of bad lighting alone obscuring the aperture. Wish we had a frontal photo.

EYE SOCKETS: Surprisingly small.

BROW RIDGE: Super massive.

FOREHEAD: Small and recessive.

HAIR or FUR: Long and black, with white around the temples and forehead. Whitening also around the throat or beard.

EARS: We cannot see them.

HEAD SHAPE: One eyewitness of the Hibagon described his head as an "inverted triangle," wide at the top and pointy at the chin. This would be the opposite of the North American bigfoot, and the opposite of the Hibagon cadaver photo. Here he has a wide Cheshire Cat mouth and jaw, and a pointy pinhead. How to explain this? I explain it two ways.
[1] Variation in individuals. To put it in terms of potatoes, my own head is a dolichocephalic Idaho potato. My wife's head is a brachiocephalic, or perfectly round Round Yellow potato. Question:

Which shape is correct for humans? A: Both are.
Supplementary Question: Which head do our two
children have? A: The elegant, nobly elongated
version, so beautiful to behold. No disrespect to
your good honest ball heads. There is variation
within species, is the point.
[2] Hairstyle. You take the same man—say, the
actor Hugh Jackman—and compare photos of him
in different films. Take him at the start of *Les
Miserables*, or in *Logan*, where he has a full beard.
His jaw looks much bigger and squarer than when
he is clean shaven. But take him in his *Wolverine*
role, and you have a man with a very V-shaped
jaw, much sharper and narrower than when clean
shaven. The bushy Wolverine hairstyle completes
the "inverted triangle" appearance. Why, you may
take *me* on Sunday morning in the pew, hair nicely
oiled and combed. Take me only two hours earlier,
waking up on the floor, hungover. The difference is
arresting.

STATE OF DECOMPOSITION: My haematologist
friend and I were puzzled by the contrast between
the bleached bones and the pristine hair or fur.
Then I found a study by a forensic entomologist, on
the outdoor decomposition of a bear carcass.
Photographs were taken over a three-month period.
Months one and two were messy with rot,
liquefaction and maggots. By month three,
everything had dried up nicely. The maggots had
gone away. The bear was a bleached skeleton,

bones poking through a pristine furry hide. It matched up with our dead Hibagon perfectly.[62]

LACK OF LARGE SCAVENGERS. Nothing disturbed this cadaver. I think the "fear and dread"[63] of the hibagon is so much on the animals that large scavengers, e.g. wild pigs, won't touch it. Think about it. The hibagon, if I am correct, is essentially a wild-pig-eating machine. A wild pig angel of death. If I were a wild pig, I'd steer well clear of them too, alive or dead.

---

[62] Joe Keiper, Ph.D., http://bugsandbear.blogspot.com/2007/05/black-bear-decomposition-week-1.html
[63] Genesis 9:2

14 THE CADAVER PHOTOS: EXPERT OPINIONS

I eventually submitted the photos to nine experts: a haematologist; a radiologist; a trauma surgeon; a pediatric surgeon; three dentists; a veterinarian; and a primatologist. The two surgeons are Canadian. The other experts are all Japanese. Dental and veterinary assistants also saw the photographs. The nine experts were asked two questions. Is this a real cadaver? What is it?

Conditions: Experts were questioned separately and confidentially. Each expert was informed of the photos' purported subject and origin. No time limit was given for answers/comments. No expert was told others' opinion until he had given his own. <u>Prior to consultation, no expert believed in the Hibagon</u>.

Concerning the first question, "Is this a real cadaver?," eight out of nine experts said YES. The dental and veterinary assistants agreed. The primatologist hemmed and hawed and never did answer.

Concerning the second question, "What is it?" no one could say. Several experts asked for time to look in reference books. The primatologist and the veterinarian took the most time (several days). Finally, eight experts gave somewhat flabby or easy-out answers, e.g. *I cannot identify it*. Or, *Unknown.* The primatologist confirmed that it is no known species of ape. The veterinarian was the bravest. "*It is neither a gorilla nor a human. **<u>It is an unidentified animal</u>**.*" [Emphasis added.]

Concerning attitudes, the primatologist was the closest thing to a hostile witness. He was perfectly courteous and generous and nice. But he was clear that he does not, and will not ever, believe in the hibagon. Yet he could not explain the photos. He just *shakes* his head.

Five experts were left *scratching* their heads, stymied.

Three experts, having the courage of their convictions, *bowed* their heads in the face of the evidence. These most hibagon-accepting and equitable gentlemen were the haematologist, the pediatric surgeon, and the veterinarian. <u>The haematologist is now a believer</u>. We are planning a trip to Mount Hiba together. <u>The pediatric surgeon leans toward believing</u>, and also wants to come. The veterinarian remains agnostic as to species, but cheerfully confirms for us that ***<u>we do have an unidentified 2-meter-tall humanoid biped running around these Chūgoku Mountains</u>***. I call this:

TRIUMPHANT, TOTAL VINDICATION

What do *you* think of these photos? Whether you are an expert or a layman, I welcome your comments. Would especially love, love, love to hear from paleontologists and facial reconstructors!

15 GOING FORWARD

With the blessing of our correct-thinking experts, I think it is possible [1] to find the skeleton; [2] to find and document living hibagon. I mean to do both.

FINDING THE SKELETON
The body was discovered somewhere "in Hibagon's usual area," and buried "nearby." This is according to the person who gave the photos to Fuji TV. But what does that mean, "Hibagon's usual area"? And just how nearby is "nearby?"
Locatable hibagon sightings form a rough triangle with an area of approximately 780 km^2. That's obviously too vast. I intend to focus on the first three official sightings. Routes 256 and 314 surround an area of some 3 km^2. I have already hiked the perimeter with Photo One in hand. One place is a possible match. I need to go back and make a careful study. I also want to look at clearings in the interior. And I might need some help from a botanist. It has been a few decades, but there is enough information in Photo One to identify the location *if I can find it*. If the location of Photo One cannot be found inside this area, then I will extend the search outward.
Once I find the location of Photo One, finding the Hibagon's grave should be relatively easy. "Nearby" means, I take it, "very nearby."
Put yourself in the farmer's shoes. You're out hunting wild mushrooms or whatever. You come across the rotting corpse of a hibagon. It's not right

to leave him lying out here. So you get a couple of
friends to help bury him.

You are not prepared for this, remember. You
don't have hazmat suits, jumbo-sized body bags, a
backhoe. If you're lucky you have work gloves,
some rope, and a couple of shovels.

You are going to find the nearest soft soil because
you don't want to be handling this corpse more than
you have to. How much do you enjoy picking up a
dead rotting rat? How about a dead rotting cat? A
dead rotting Labrador Retriever?

You don't want to drag it far. It might break apart,
and then you'd have to go back and pick up broken
pieces and so on. This thing is dirty, stinky, and
possibly infectious. You want to get it underground
as fast as possible.

How deep do we dig, if we are these farmers? Not
very. Humans don't do more work than we have to,
especially when the work is unpleasant. We have
tree roots to deal with… Hey, you know what? This
thing is mostly decomposed already anyway...
Nobody is going to find it anyway... We never
asked for this job anyway… Let's just do this and
be done with it. Make that grave as shallow as we
can get away with. Two hibagon thicknesses
should do it. That deflated corpse looks about 30-
40 cm thick to me.

Now the scene might be greatly changed after 30
or 40 years. There might be a tree growing over the
Hibagon. Or it might not have changed all that
much. We won't know until we find it.

If we are really lucky—well, this is what I am hoping: My father-in-law was from this area. Whenever his dogs died, he buried them. Then he erected gravestones and left offerings. That's what Japanese do for the dead. By roadsides, wherever cars have killed people, you see little stone idols, and flowers, and cans of coffee, and bottles of tea. One place on the way up to my parents-in-law's farm, there was an old human sacrifice. We're talking fairly long ago. A girl was slain for good luck before the building of a dam. The farmers still leave flowers.

So I'm hoping that our farmer/gravediggers left a bottle of sake, or a bottle of beer, or something else that survived. If we are really lucky they might have left a little cairn or something. Also, please pray with me that the grave is on public land. If it is on public land, I can dig. And if I find it underground, by Japanese law, it belongs to me. I know the law because I do metal detecting. Here in my city there are 50 sites of old castles. Fifty, within city limits! One that I really love is on top of a mountain. No one knows it's there. It was the scene of two battles, 600 years ago. On my first trip I found a bronze *menuki,* a decorative charm from a samurai sword. Beautiful. Still has tiny sparkles of gold overlay. This thing is under an inch long. I found it in 20 minutes, 5 or 6 inches down. Because no one else bothered to look for it. This gives me hope. If a man can find an inch-long menuki from 600 years ago, that man can find a 2-meter hibagon skeleton.

FINDING LIVING HIBAGON

Fifty years ago we had a breeding population of hibagon. Are any still there? It would be very, very surprising if this apex omnivore, this king of the forest, went extinct in my brief lifetime. Besides, I can't think of a single challenge that hibagon might have now, that wasn't worse in the 70s and 80s. Humans are not encroaching. The countryside is depopulating.[64] Hibagon have no predators. Japan has almost no hunters. Hibagon food is more abundant than ever.[65] AND. I think they are still there because they are still taking people. Still, here and there, shooting out their long hairy arms where the bush grows thick and close beside the trail.

I am making autumn trips to Mount Hiba every year for the rest of my life. Why autumn? Because it is a peak time for hibagon sightings, and also a peak time for humans mysteriously disappearing in this prefecture. This is what I do:

I carry a 16" hunting knife. Can't have even a simple shotgun in this country, and a knife is better than nothing. I cook outdoors, hoping to lure curious hibagon in. I sit outside as late as I can. I do not sleep outside. I keep a little fire going. I speak into the woods, in English and Japanese.

---

[64] In rural depopulation Japan is third, behind Bulgaria and Albania.

[65] Nippon.com: "Wild Boar Boom: Animal Encroachment a Growing Concern for Rural Communities." South China Morning Post: "Wild boars are taking over Japan's small towns, and residents are either too old or too few to scare them away.

Tell them I mean no harm, and I wish to see them. I sometimes play music at low volume. I try to keep a digital audio recorder going all the time. I sometimes smoke a pipe. I wear regular outdoor clothes (trousers, tweed jacket, that sort of thing). I hike around, but I don't expect to find hibagon in the woods. My hope is for hibagon to come to me.

But it is good to get into those woods. Last year I found teepee-frame multipod stick structures, with 5 or 6 sticks arranged in a cone, and woven together at the peak. I took photos and showed them around to area people. No one could tell me who made them or for what purpose. A farmer could have made them, but then you would expect other farmers to be able to recognize them. Anyway, it is certain that making these stick structures is not customary for farmers in this area.

I found them off trail, hundreds of meters or yards from the nearest house. Japanese farmers are old (average age 66). They are old and busy. They sometimes go into the bush to hunt for mushrooms and wild herbs. But they go in, do their business, and come out. They don't generally take precious time, and waste precious energy, to gather sticks and weave elaborate structures. For what? To mark a territory? But no other farmer reads this bizarre semiology. Area farmers saw *no meaning* in my photos. To play a prank? These farmers are serious characters. And how could they expect an obliging rube to stumble upon their structures, deep in the bush? Besides, no one in Japan has any idea that bigfoot make conical teepee-frame stick structures in North America. No one in this area, certainly. No one but me.

I am saving my photos for a future book (I hope) filled with physical evidence gathered, and new information learned, on my biannual expeditions to Mount Hiba.

Last year (2020) my daughters and I were preoccupied with researching my sea monster. We started a little organization, called the Tomonoura Organization for Monster Observance (TOMO). This year (2021) we want to start a sister group. We are calling it the Hibayama Organization for Monster Observance.[66]

---

[66] HOMO, a salute to our shared DNA. Bigfoot/hibagon are not animals. They are a kind of people. They have language. See the work of US Navy cryptolinguist Scott Nelson on bigfoot language. See also David Paulides' Hoopa Project. See also the work of Dr. Melba Ketchum et al. "Our data indicate that the North American Sasquatch is a hybrid species, the result of males of an unknown hominin species crossing with female Homo sapiens." [National Post, Nov 28, 2012: "Bigfoot real and the result of human women mating with an 'unknown hominin,' claims U.S. study"] See again Seraphine Long and others. American Indian tribes always considered them people. In Chinese, the word yeren includes the character for man. They can breed with us (and do). This is why Dr Ketchum says "Government at all levels must recognize them as an indigenous people and immediately protect their human and Constitutional rights against those who would see in their physical and cultural differences a 'license' to hunt, trap, or kill them." Since 2013, bigfoot has had a species name waiting for it. ZooBank has approved Dr Ketchum's registration request for the name *Homo sapiens cognatus*." "Cognatus" means "related by blood."

16 REMAINING QUESTIONS

I have about a million billion remaining questions, but here are three.

Q: What provoked the rash of sightings 1970-1982?

Starting with the standard Lone Hibagon narrative, I thought we were dealing with a rogue juvenile male. Maybe an outcast male. This would account for his sudden appearance, and his growth from 160 cm to 2 meters. Then I found the footprint data. Adjustment: It could be an outcast family, or a split-off family that relocated. It could be a forced relocation. Forced by external events.

The primary industry here is mining. Shokozan Mining Co., Ltd. (Japan's biggest miner of limestone) began pit mining in the area in 1959. In 1964 they completed their first dry factory, for crushing pyrophyllite. A second dry factory was completed in March, 1968. This is a complex on the Saijo River. The Geibi train line runs right by. Across the river is forest. It stretches unbroken 22 kilometers north, clear to Mount Hiba.[67] Maybe this factory pushed a group out of here. Maybe it was loggers.

Or how about a construction megaproject? The 4-lane Chūgoku Expressway slices through Hiroshima Prefecture east to west. It runs 20 km

---

[67] Hiking in a straight line today, you would have to cross a total of 6 lonely country roads.

south of Mount Hiba, just south of Shobara City, and wraps around it. Construction chewed through a lot of forests, and blasted miles and miles of tunnels. The highway was begun in 1964, and opened in 1970. Fits our timeline. Did some of that dynamite go off too close to a hibagon hole? Force them out, ears ringing, brains scrambled, and suddenly homeless? Mount Hiba's virgin off-limits-to-logging forests would have offered the perfect escape.

Once relocated, well you know how it is. *You* ever moved to a new city? These hibagon are going to make mistakes at first. Until they learn the lay of the land, the habits and movements of pigs and people. As time goes by they settle in, and people see them less and less. That is precisely what the record shows.

Q: What *are* hibagon/bigfoot?

I think they're a kind of people. See my footnote to HOMO. They may not be people as we understand people, but hey. It is coming out that some groups of mankind have between 0.5 and 3% Neanderthal DNA, while other groups have none. Yet others have up to 20% of Homo erectus DNA, and others none. *It turns out that even people aren't all people in quite the same way.*

The bigfoot/hibagon share DNA with us. This has been proven in the laboratory, and proven in the field. If someone can rape you and make you pregnant, he has to share a lot of DNA with you.

Now you share 60% of your DNA with bananas, but you can't breed with a banana. You share 98.7% with chimps, and I don't know if people can breed with chimps. I don't know if it's ever been tried and tested. I hope not, but knowing human nature I guess it has been tried both in the field and in the laboratory. You share 99.9% with the man in the street, and the man in the street definitely can rape you and make you pregnant. So I guess the bigfoot/hibagon is somewhere between a 98.7% and a 99.9% match.

The haematologist and I have looked at hundreds of skulls. The closest we can find to our Fuji TV friend is the Paranthropus or Paranthropids: *Paranthropus robustus, and Paranthropus boisei.*

These are supposed to be pre-humans or proto-humans that lived millions and billions of years ago. I would rather call them *para*-humans, from Gr. *para*: *beside, near, resembling, or adjacent.* Do an image search on these guys. Compare their skulls with our friend's. The jawbones and teeth size, shape, and number are the same.[68] Look at artists' reconstructions, and look again at our hibagon police sketch. Allow for sexual dimorphism, families, individual looks, hairstyles, medieval oysters, and all of that. Keep in mind that artists

---

[68] Note that the Paranthropids had a low incidence rate of tertiary dentin (which helps to repair tooth damage), and high rates of pitting enamel hypoplasia, dental cavities, tooth loss, and periodontal disease. In a sample of 15 specimens, all of them had bone loss from gum disease. Compare with our hibagon skull.

don't know how hairy these things were, or what hair and skin colours they had.

Better, look at the sketches by police forensic artist, Harvey Pratt. Some of those faces could go right over our Fuji TV skull. They are very human faces.

That's my best guess. Bigfoot/hibagon are *P. robustus* and/or *P. boisei*, and/or similar strains of para-humans.[69] They had/have the midtarsal break.[70] Some groups must have had genes for gigantism switched on; others not. Other observed differences are racial, sexual, etc.

---

[69] I came to this theory independently, by looking at pictures of skulls. I did not know that, "Primatologist John R. Napier and anthropologist Gordon Strasenburg have suggested a species of Paranthropus as a possible candidate for Bigfoot's identity, such as Paranthropus robustus, with its gorilla-like crested skull and bipedal gait—despite the fact that fossils of Paranthropus are found only in Africa." The last bit is hardly an objection as conditions for fossilization are so rare. And anyway, bigfoot probably bury their dead. Strasenburgh wrote a book entitled "Paranthropus: Once and Future Brother," and many articles, e.g. "On Paranthropus and Relic Humanoids." Dr Melba Ketchum has spoken favourably of the Paranthropus theory, and Cliff Barackman has adopted it. Michael Rugg of the Bigfoot Discovery Museum proposes another hominin, called Meganthropus, who overlaps somehow with Homo erectus. Meganthropus comes out of Asia. I wonder what any of these researchers will make of the Fuji TV photos.

[70] D. Jeffrey Meldrum, "Midfoot Flexibility, Fossil Footprints, and Sasquatch Steps: New Perspectives on the Evolution of Bipedalism," Journal of Scientific Exploration, March 2004.

You can guess where I stand on the kill/no-kill question. Koko the gorilla knew 2000 English words. She was able to communicate with American Sign Language. She had an IQ of 75 or so. Take a look at an IQ map of the world. Some *countries* average lower IQs than that. I have some low IQ friends and neighbours, and I'm not for killing them. I certainly wouldn't kill Koko the gorilla. So no, I don't approve of killing bigfoot/hibagon except in self-defence.

Q: Why are they taking people?

We know that they used to take people for food and forced reproduction. Both motives may be behind abductions today.

Out of Hiroshima's 26 current NPA cases, 3 involved sexually viable (post pubertal, premenopausal) women. Weirdly in this highly homogenous nation, only one of these women was Japanese.[71] None of the other 23 victims were foreigners. I don't know what to make of this. Perhaps, and this is just a thought I am throwing out, if human-women abductions were fueled by a powerful drive for exogamy, foreign women might be even more desirable?

Sex seems not to be the primary motive anyway, as most victims are elderly, and more than half of the victims are men. So it seems as if they're taking us mainly for food.

---

[71] One was Chinese, and one Brazilian.

But they don't take us very often. We're far from
their main meal. Seasonality of abductions lines up
very well with seasonality of known hibagon
sightings. Abductions peak in autumn and early
winter. They stop completely in January and
February, when snowy footprints could lead men
with guns to mountain hideaways. Then begin
again in March. They die down in late spring and
summer, when food resources are most abundant.

But I do not want to underestimate our
hibagon/bigfoot neighbours. They are intelligent.
Some of them, at least, have language. Do they
have culture? Oral tradition? Rites and religion? I
hold out the following possibilities.

They may simply hate us. They may feel
aggrieved. They may have long memories. They
may tell and retell times we have done them wrong.

They may have a rite of passage. As a Bushman
has his initiation antelope hunt, so an adolescent
hibagon might be tasked with bringing home one of
us.

Perhaps the hibagon deity demands blood and
meat.

Maybe human meat to them is something like a
Christmas turkey to us: a special dish for special
occasions. Birthdays, feast days, and so on.

Maybe they hunt us for sport. The thrill of the kill.

Maybe wearing a human head or scalp on your
belt is a hibagon status symbol.

Maybe producing a human trophy grants a
hibagon expanded sexual access.

Maybe they make us into throw rugs.

Maybe they use our organs for medicine, much as the Chinese use bear bile or rhinoceros horns as aphrodisiacs.

Maybe they would never eat us for themselves. Personally, they'd rather die of starvation. But when it comes down to one of us, or one of their own starving children, the equation changes. Maybe they think they are doing us a favour by choosing the smallest and frailest and weakest. Maybe they understand that the elderly victims will lose the least years. Maybe they know that we don't even seem to miss the elderly much. We don't look for them all that hard. Maybe the hibagon weeps for his own victims, the way I wept when I would skin a rabbit for Hasenpfeffer.

Maybe it's a compulsion he can't control, a kind of Jekyll and Hyde thing. Maybe he hates himself for it, and beats himself up in the morning. Maybe he cries to his hiba-god to save him from his terrible addiction. Maybe *his* dreams are haunted by the faces of people that *we've* long since forgotten. Maybe he thinks *we're* kind of being the insensitive assholes. I don't know, I'm not a hibapsychologist.

I know one thing. Looking down on these beings as dumb apes has gotten us nowhere toward understanding them.

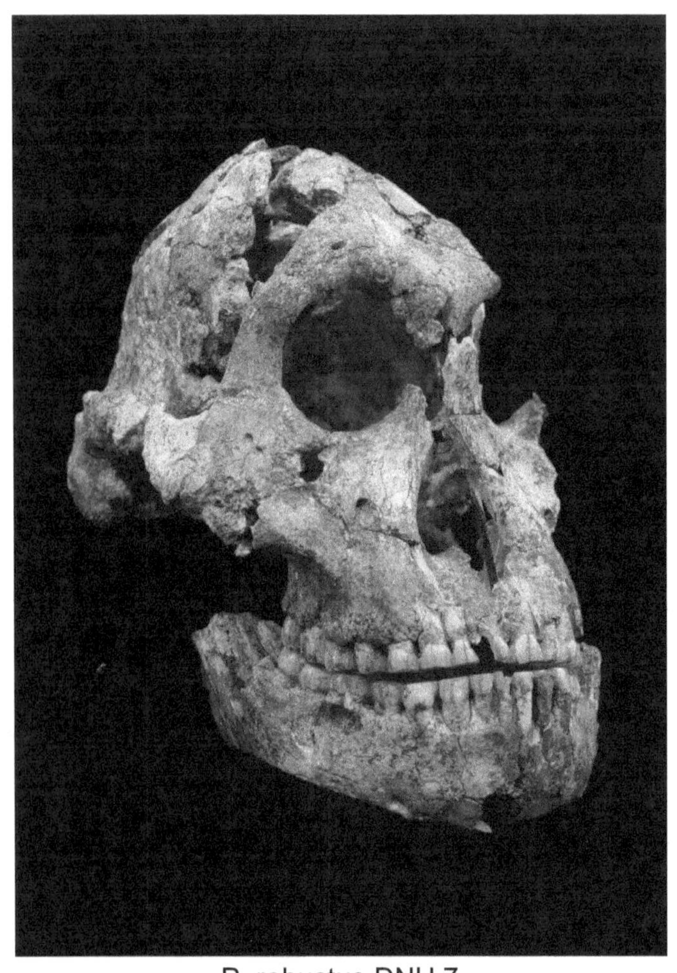

P. robustus DNH 7
Compare with the second Fuji TV photo

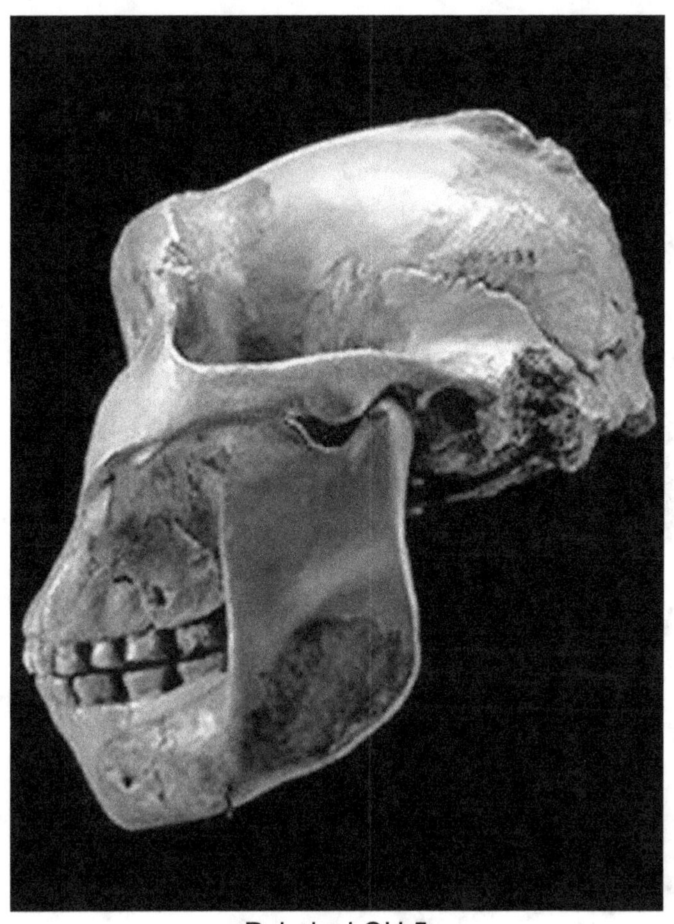

P. boisei OH 5
Compare with the second Fuji TV photo

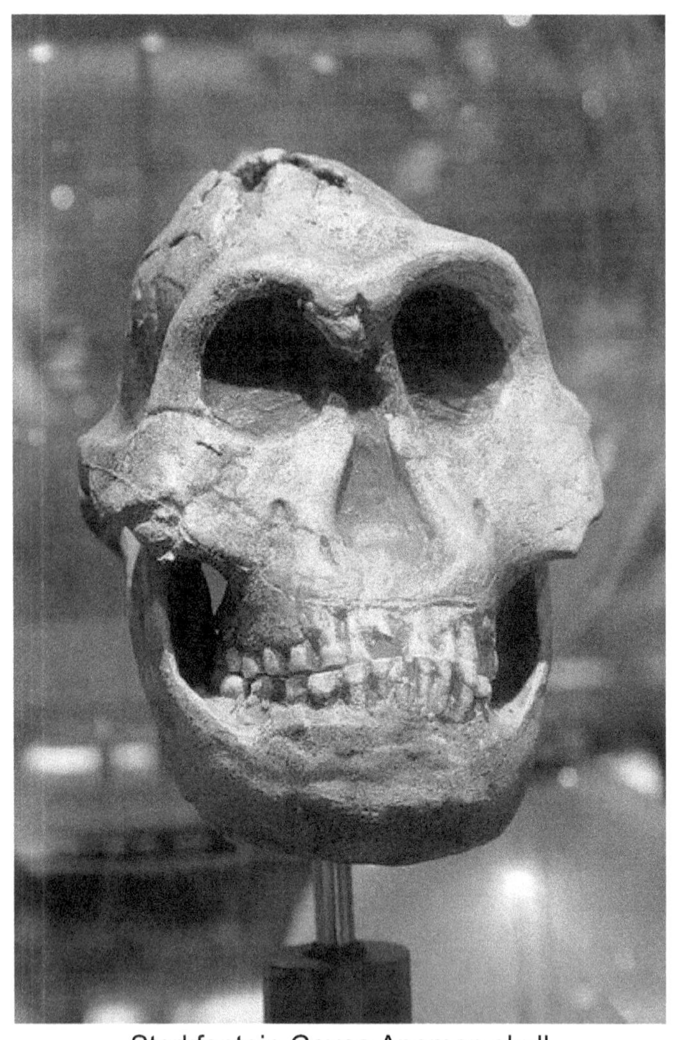

Sterkfontein Caves Apeman skull
Compare with the second Fuji TV photo

Two artists' reconstructions of
P. boisei. One more apelike, one more human.

P. hibagonsus?

17 CONCLUSION

The Hibagon, a.k.a. *enko, satori, kakusaru* or *jueyuan, ikemono,* etc. is the Japanese bigfoot. These people or creatures are real. Based on eyewitness evidence alone, they are real.

Some super-duper tough skeptics will never accept this. "Not till I see a body on a slab." Very well. We have brought him a body, photographed close-up. It fully satisfies eight out of nine experts, and even the hostile ninth cannot debunk it. Somehow I fear that even this will fail to satisfy some stubborn fools.

It doesn't matter. On our side are university research teams, the Hiroshima Police, the Ape Clerk, physicians, dentists, veterinarians, and one very reluctant primatologist. Most of all, *we* are on the side of the dozens and dozens of eyewitnesses here in Hiroshima Prefecture, and the tens of thousands around the world. Involuntary, traumatised, ridiculed, courageous eyewitnesses:

I believe you.

We have ongoing evidence. People continue to go missing precisely in those parts of Japan with histories of hibagon-type presences. Nara, Hiroshima, Yamaguchi, Gifu, Niigata, Ishikawa, Gunma… it's not stopping.

Please watch for my next book, **Missing Japan: Hiroshima**. There I will make the case that a forest/mountain predator is taking people, with hibagon the chief suspect. This book will be out later this year (2021) or early next year. When it is done, I will take a copy to the Hiroshima Police. I will ask for someone to sit down and discuss this with me. Can't wait to tell you how that goes!

Maybe I can tell you about it in my *next* book, **Missing Japan: Chūgoku**. This will look at cases surrounding Hiroshima, in the other prefectures that make up the Chūgoku region: Yamaguchi, Tottori, Shimane, and Okayama. Also cases across the Seto Inland Sea, in Kagawa and Ehime.

Then on to *Gifu* and adjacent prefectures, and then *Niigata* and adjacent prefectures, etc. I will also talk about these cases on YouTube, on the **Brink Books** channel.

Meanwhile, local fieldwork must continue. I hope to make annual springtime trips looking for the Fuji TV cadaver, and autumn trips looking for live hibagon. Thank you for reading, and once more, I will say:

よろしくお願ねがいします.

Write: **brink.and.daughters@gmail.com**
Subscribe on YouTube: **Brink Books**

Buy me a day in the bush! I am on Paypal as Kyle Brink, with a fine portrait of me painted by my godson. I am dressed as a Spanish conquistador. I am twiddling my moustache.

YOU

can help me be the Jane Goodall of the hibagon.

APPENDIX 1:
An Imaginary Conversation between Mrs Lucy Thompson and Hiroko, a Japanese Peasant Wife.

HIROKO

Welcome, please sit down. Please forgive all the confusion in our village. An enko was spotted on the mountainside this morning. Enko or oni. In your language, I think you call it a devil.

LUCY

The Klamath Indians say that from the creation of man until the present day, some were made to be good and honourable, some bad, and some real bad and mean, which they termed devils, or Oh-ma-ha.

HIROKO

Is it a spirit or a flesh-and-blood creature?

LUCY

A real living devil such as walks the earth, and we fear them as they will harm us if they get the opportunity. We have had these living Indian devils all through the long and weary centuries, ever since the creation of mankind.

HIROKO

Yes, we have those devils here in Japan. Please tell me more about your devils.

LUCY

In their loneliness they roam through the forests and over the mountains like some wild animals of prey. They forget the language of their mothers and become

something like wild beasts, fleeing from the sight of
human beings.

HIROKO
Ours do the same. Please go on.

LUCY
In olden times, the women especially were always
careful to keep together on their camping trips when they
were gathering the acorn crop, grass seeds, pine nuts,
etc., for fear of these Indian devils. These Indian devils
would sometimes watch the camps of the Indians very
closely and follow them about as they moved from place
to place, watching for an opportunity to seize one of the
young women and carry her off to make her his wife. If a
young woman strayed away too far by herself, she was
often made a captive by one of these devils. The women
of the tribe had a great fear of them as they had great
horrors of becoming the wife of a wild man.

HIROKO
Oh, it's the same with our devils. A woman can't go
anywhere alone. I heard that in Gifu, one of these devils
reached up through the toilet. Tried to snatch a poor
woman right out through the toilet! They take women
and keep them. They even make babies with them.

LUCY
Sometimes the women would be captivated by the
Indian devils and would be gone away from their tribe for
years, when they would return and tell of their wild life
and experiences. They would become the mother of
children, and the children would inherit the wild habits of
their father, as they would always be whistling, making

strange noises, romping wildly about and always on the
go, roaming everywhere in the wilds.

HIROKO

They are very bad, these devils. One of our captured
women came home with child. When the child was born,
it was a monster! Well it had to be burned of course,
poor thing. Did you know that they use the riverbed to
sneak into town at night? When it suits them, they can
go on all fours, just like animals. They're very crafty.

LUCY

When the Indians would go on their hunting and
camping trips into the mountains, as soon as they heard
an owl screech or hoot, they would stop and listen, and
try to distinguish if it was an Indian devil imitating the owl
or the cry of a wild animal. The Indians would stop at
once, kindle a fire and hallo; this was given as a warning
to the devils that they were awake and ready to fight
them if necessary.

HIROKO

Sometimes they pretend to be crying babies. They cry
just like little helpless babies! Of course they want to fool
you, so you go out in the woods, and then they take you.
When they try that trick we call them *kawaakago*. Well,
our men will keep bonfires burning tonight. They'll keep
watch. We ladies will pray, and chant the sutras, and
burn incense.

LUCY

When the Indians go camping far back into the
mountains, even if a white man accompanies them, they
always insist on making the first campfire when a

camping place is selected. In building the fire, the first stick of wood they lay down directly north and south. On the north end of this stick they place another stick some eight or twelve inches back from the north end, placing this branch east and west, thus making a cross. When the cross is made, they proceed to kindle the fire, and during the whole time they are offering up a prayer to God in a low tone of voice. This prayer is earnestly offered up to the Almighty asking Him to protect them from the Indian devils.[72]

HIROKO
We have an oni exorcism ritual that works wonders—but look at me! Where are my manners? You just rest here, and I am going to go and put on the kettle. Some nice green tea to settle our nerves, that's what we need...

---

[72] Lucy's words are her own, from Chapter 9, Indian Devils. I also like Chapter 23, The Romance of a Wild Indian. Agree with her or not, Mrs Thompson's opinions are always interesting, whether she is applauding her tribe's enslavement of Hoopas and Klamath-Hoopa half breeds, or decreeing that any woman who suffers a miscarraiage should be forever shamed and ostracized. I also love her unquestioning chauvinism. "The Klamath Indians are the best in the world at handling their women in childbirth, in the old Indian way." And her somewhat gleeful accounts of murders, by Klamath Indians, of innocent white men. I am quite taken with this book and may have to republish it myself, with helpful annotations, and of course at a reasonable price.

APPENDIX 2:
Mysteriously Missing Persons
Prefectural Rates per 100,000
(NPA data July, 2021)

Tokyo	.000
Shiga	.000
Kochi	.000
Saga	.000
Okinawa	.000
Nagano	.048
Okayama	.052
Fukushima	.055
Kumamoto	.057
Chiba	.063
Hokkaido	.075
Saitama	.081
Miyazaki	.093
Fukuoka	.097
Ibaraki	.104
Yamanashi	.122
Fukui	.128
Tokushima	.137
Kyoto	.156
Oita	.176
Kanagawa	.187
Hyogo	.219
MEAN	.264

.... start of 1st standard deviation

Shizuoka	.274
Nagasaki	.304
Wakayama	.317
Aomori	.320
Osaka	.328
Aichi	.344
Mie	.366
Tochigi	.411
Kagoshima	.437

Miyagi	.520
Tottori	.525
Yamagata	.555
Kagawa	.526
.... start of 2nd standard deviation	
Iwate	.569
Shimane	.601
Toyama	.670
Ishikawa	.701
Akita	.724
Gifu	.753
Niigata	.763
Gunma	.774
Yamaguchi	.871
.... start of 3rd standard deviation	
Ehime	.894
Hiroshima	.924
.... start of 4th standard deviation	
Nara	1.361

I'm not a statistician, but my friend the haematologist is. Pharmaceutical corporations trust him to manage major drug trials. So I took these numbers to him. And I brought him my problem.

Measure almost any human feature or phenomenon, chart it out, and you will come up with a graph shaped like a bell or an arch. The familiar bell curve. Something like this:

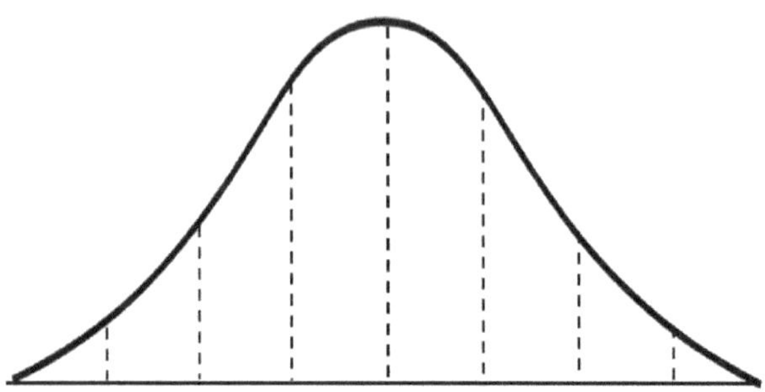

Where most of the population clumps around the mean in the centre. Because whether you look at human IQ, or height, or weight, or length of noses, or what have you, most people are near the average. Most people have an average length of nose. You have at the far left the Phantom of the Opera, and at the far right Cyrano. But such outliers are rare.

Similarly, if you measure US states or cities, or Japanese prefectures, for human phenomena such as crime rates, wealth, cancer rates, accidents, suicides, rates of tertiary education, etc. you will have a prefecture with the lowest rate, and a prefecture with the highest rate. Most prefectures will lump around the middle. Distribution will be narrow. The hump will be high and squeezed at the sides. Why? Because in all of these states and cities and prefectures, for all their differences, we are still looking at humans. Humans have a human nature that gravitates toward the centre.

Look again at the chart. If this measures IQ, then the centre line represents 100. Each section to the right is an increase of 15 points. So the first section (standard deviation) to the right covers IQs of 101 to 115. The second standard deviation covers IQs of 116 to 130. The third covers IQs of 131 to 145. They decrease in size as you would expect. Genius is rare.

But what if we chart the NPA data? I have made a simple line graph. We get a list of 47 prefectures along the □ axis, with Tokyo (and four other .000 prefectures) at the far left, and Nara at the far right. Starting from the left, we have a long, very gentle ramp up to the centre line. You could sit in a wheelchair and power yourself up with almost no effort, this ramp is so gentle. If you were adding a colour code, you could colour the entire left side green for safety, perhaps turning green-yellow toward the centre.

Crossing the centre line, our line steps up in 1, 2, 3, 4 steps, coloured yellow, orange, pink, and red. And then a fifth great leap up to glowing and flashing red Nara.

Now imagine this is a bell chart. The population balloons up into a vertical bulbous tumour all on the right side. If this were an IQ chart it would represent a population made up exclusively of geniuses and imbeciles, with almost no one of average intelligence. There is no central hump. The hump is all on the right. It looks like a certain horrid big slug-like galactic crime lord.

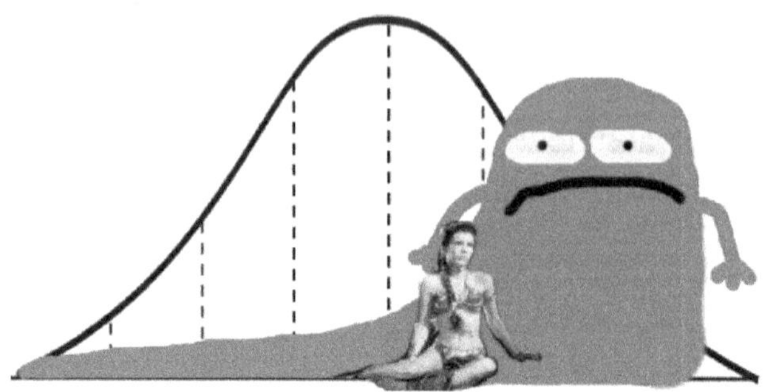

  Now in all of these NPA cases, the police have ruled out crime, suicide, accident, voluntary disappearance, and every other human occurence. That's why they're appealing for help. Because they have nothing like it in their experience.

  Our right-sided, accelerating hump chart confirms this. All of the above human phenomena chart like a bell. To the haematologist and me, this confirms that we are not looking at a *non-human* phenomenon. *Homo sapiens sapiens* are not doing this. *Homo sapiens sapiens* are not running this show.

Please look forward to
Missing Japan: Hiroshima
Also in the works:

A Guide to Tomonoura
Clothing in the Bible
Infertility, God, & DMSO
Megaliths of Japan
Metal Detecting in Japan
Sasquatch in Paradise
The Angry Banana's Best Bedtime Stories
The Kokeshi Conspiracy
Timmy's Big Book of Prepositions
Tomosaurus: Sea Serpent of Tomonoura

Till next time,

よろしくお願ねがいします.

INDEX